First Tracks

TABLE OF CONTENTS

D1591364

DEDICATION

This book is dedicated to my father who instilled in me a love of skiing and to my mother who inspired me to write about it.

Acknowledgements

It is impossible to properly acknowledge here everyone who helped me with the research for this book. Many people told me stories, gave me names to follow up with or suggested new directions to research. I thank all those who assisted me in documenting these stories from Maine's skiing heritage.

I also want to thank Mason Beekley, Morten Lund, Doug Pfeiffer and Janet Nelson who have all helped me become a ski history writer.

Nicholas Noyes and Holly Hurd-Forsyth from the Maine Historical Society helped me research the Society's collection. Holly found the photos of the 1924 Portland Winter Carnival in the not well marked collection of 15,000 negatives.

Tom Gaffney and Thomas Bennett from the Portland Room at the Portland Public Library assisted with my research in that collection.

Thanks go to Annie Darling, the creative designer, she is responsible for the design, layout and computer production of the book; and to Kevin Brusie who created the digital photography work, including photo retouching of old photos which had deteriorated. Carole Taylor did the proofreading; she enjoys pointing out my mistakes.

Morten Lund and Earline Marsh assisted me with the editing. Both offered valuable advice and helped direct me to the strong points of the stories.

Mike Reynolds, executive director of Ski Maine, and the rest of the Ski Maine members made this book possible. Mike allowed me to develop my idea and write the book with all the assistance I needed but in the direction and style that I wanted. They have been this writer's ideal publisher.

Donna, my wife, cheerfully joined me on research trips, put up with my early morning writing before I left for my real job and listened to my stories as they developed. I offer her my biggest thanks.

Decal from a Paris Manufacturing ski from the early 1930s.

1

It was one of those fall days that makes you long for the departing warm days of summer but still carries with it the excitement of the coming winter. Outside the lodge of the old Big A ski area on top of Mount Agamenticus, birders were watching the fall migration of hawks. Red-tailed, sharp-shinned and broad-winged hawks, along with osprey and kestrels, used the thermals of the coastal mountain to help their southern migration. We hiked the ski trails and photographed rusty lift towers. Hillsides were in their full, glorious, fall colors and the Atlantic Ocean a few miles east added its own beauty.

Donna, my wife, and I had packed a cooler of food and along with our two dogs were exploring southern Maine looking for old ski areas. I used my collection of ski magazines and Maine ski guides to locate several on the map, and now we wanted to find them, climb the trails and try to feel the history. We started the day at Rotary Park in Biddeford, the site of a small community rope tow. The tow path was clearly visible but the tow itself was gone. In addition to Rotary Park and Big A, we wanted to find Spring Hill, Beaver Hill and Ossipee Mountain ski areas.

In the 1930s there had been a rope tow in North Berwick operated by the Bauneg Beg Ski Club. Over sixty years had passed and it was unlikely that we would find any sign of the ski slope, but we wanted to try. On a back road we passed kids selling pumpkins, waved and drove past. In their back yard we saw a steep hillside cleared of trees with what looked like a rope tow. We backed up and asked the kids what that was. "It's my Daddy's rope tow," one of them said. Daddy, Richard Legere, was on his tractor enlarging the pond at the base of the hill.

Legere had bought the Rotary Park rope tow from the city of Biddeford, rebuilt it and installed it on his own hillside. The pond he was expanding was for his snowmaking system.

Legere's ski area, Bauneg Beg Ski Trails, is Maine's newest ski area and yet in some ways it goes back in time to the soul of Maine skiing. It is a small area that requires an enormous amount of work from a small, dedicated, group of people. Family and friends are those who benefit. Why does he do it? "I love to ski," Legere answers.

I have traveled Maine, from York to Madawaska, researching Maine's skiing heritage, and people have told me that a love of the sport and having fun are the reasons they devoted the time and effort needed to create a ski trail or an area. Mainers love to be outside in all seasons, and they especially appreciate the beauty of winter.

I stood in a potato field in Fort Fairfield while August Harvey, a potato farmer, sat on his tractor, pointed at nearby White Bunny ski area and told me stories from the time he worked there. Alden Anderson and Harold Bondeson, from New Sweden, told me about the ski marathons they raced in during the 1930s. Avon Hilton, a racer and later a ski instructor, told me about climbing Ossipee Mountain for a high school race in 1937.

Skiing dawned in Maine in the winter of 1870-71. It was strictly utilitarian, a way to get around in the deep snows. The development of skiing into sport has had many twists and turns throughout the years. Skiing in Maine has paralleled and at times led the growth of the sport nationwide.

First Tracks is by no means a comprehensive history of skiing in Maine; it offers a look at the people and the events that have shaped Maine's skiing heritage. We will look in some detail at a few of the stories from before World War II that best illustrate the growth of skiing into a popular sport. We will also look at each of the ski areas that skiers have enjoyed in Maine.

Today, Maine offers cross country skiing on both natural and groomed trails, snowboarding, some of the best terrain, fastest lifts, and best snowmaking to be found anywhere. Maine also offers skiing as it was in the past. Homemade donuts, T-bars, areas within walking distance for the kids and trails that twist and turn with the mountain are still a part of Maine skiing.

Glenn

The Skidor Arrive

IN MAY, 1870, THOMAS SAILED

FOR SWEDEN TO OFFER 100 ACRES

OF LAND TO ANY SWEDE WILLING

TO SETTLE IN MAINE.

In the mid

1800s the Maine legislature sought to populate the vast forests of northern Maine. It offered free land to anyone who would take up the challenge of homesteading in this wilderness.

"Before 1870 the primeval forest covered all the land, stretching way over hill and dale as far as the eye could reach," wrote Widgery Thomas, state legislator and ex-Ambassador to Sweden. "No habitation of civilized man had ever been erected in these vast northern woods; through their branches the smoke from a settler's cabin had never curled; in their depths the blows from a settler's ax had never resounded. Here roamed the moose and prowled the bear, and here the silence of midnight was broken by the hooting of the arctic owl." Thomas suggested that the offer of free land be made to people in Sweden. "Would they make good citizens, these people of the north?" Thomas asked. "Yes, no one doubted that tall, stout, hardy race are these Northmen; inured to hardship, patient of labor, economical, religious and honest."

In May, 1870, Thomas sailed for Sweden to offer 100 acres of land to any Swede willing to settle in Maine. Certificates of character were required. Thomas himself had to approve each recruit. On July 23, 1870 Thomas and his group of 22 men, 11 women and 18 children arrived at a site in the woods north of Caribou. "We called the spot New Sweden," wrote Thomas, "A name at once commemorative of the past and auspicious of the future.

"Every Swede was convinced that just the right lot had fallen to him and was enabled to find something or other about his new possession which in his eye made it superior to all others. The following day the Swedes commenced the great work of converting a forest into a home."

The state was to provide the settlers not only with land but also homes and roads linking the settlement. The Swedes were paid $1 a day to cut the roads and to build their own log homes. Land was cleared and turnips, winter wheat and rye were planted.

Ullr, shown above, is a Nordic Saint and protector of skiers

Inset Left: Widgery Thomas, founder of New Sweden.
NEW SWEDEN HISTORICAL MUSEUM

A Swedish lady in traditional dress.

"Once riding out of the woods," wrote Thomas, "I met one of our Swedish women walking in with a heavy sack on her back. As she passed I noticed a commotion inside the sack.

'What have you got in there?' said I. 'Four nice pigs,' she replied. 'Where did you get the pigs?' 'Down river, two miles below Caribou.'

Children in New Sweden skied up to five miles to attend school using the traditional Swedish ski design of two different length skis.

"Two miles below Caribou was ten miles from New Sweden. So this good wife had walked 20 miles with four pigs on her back, smiling all the way to think what nice pigs they were.

"The state of Maine extended a helping hand to this infant colony and guarded it with fostering care. But in so doing the state only helped those who helped themselves. The Swedes did not come to us as paupers. The Swedish immigrants have all paid their own passage from Sweden to Maine. So healthy was the climate of our northern woods that for one year there was not a day of sickness of man, woman or child.

"The winter of 1870-71 was safely, and comfortably passed by the Swedes in these woods. They were accustomed to cold weather and deep snow. The snow lingered late that winter. Weeks after it had disappeared in the nearest villages, it still covered our new clearings in the woods."

Indians used snowshoes to get around in the deep snows. Those who followed learned to use snowshoes. The Swedes, however, knew how to build and use skidor or skis.

The skis were of the kind used in the mountain region of Norway, Sweden and Finland, unequal in length. The terrain around New Sweden was very similar. Originally there was a considerable difference in the length of the skis. The shorter ski, the andur, was used to push and the longer ski to glide on. The result was much like a kid riding a scooter. By the time New Sweden was settled the skis had become more equal in length.

The long ski was up to ten feet long with the andur being only about six inches shorter. The binding was a leather toe loop. The uneven length made the skis more stable for skiing through drifts.

Many people made skis for their own use, but a few also sold skis. Ski-makers such as Lars Stadig and Anselm Carlstrom decorated their skis with their own distinctive markings. All the skis from New Sweden in the 1800s have a long carved tip that looks like the prow of a Viking sailing ship. The shape of the tip also made it easy to anchor a rope so a pair of skis could be bound together and towed with goods on them. Skis from New Sweden were considered to be the best quality and were sought after until World War II.

Everyone in New Sweden used skis. Children skied up to five miles to attend school. Alden Anderson, who was born in New Sweden in 1920, recalls, "If you wanted to go anywhere in the winter you just jumped on your skis and went."

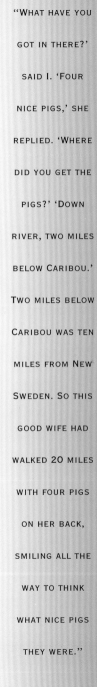

Dope is King

DOPE, OR WAX, MADE THE DIFFERENCE

BETWEEN WINNING AND LOSING FOR SKI

RACERS IN THE GOLD MINING CAMPS.

"Dope is King,"

said the posters. Dope, or wax, made the difference between winning and losing for the ski racers in the California gold mining camps. Not only were bragging rights at stake but the prizes were often equal to a year's wages.

Eighteen-year-old Frank Stewart left Skowhegan, Maine in 1851 to find gold in the California mountains. In winter, snow was so deep in the Sierra Nevadas miners used Norwegian snowshoes, known today as skis, to get around. In 1857 Stewart entered one of the first "longboard" races. Thereafter, Stewart won so often that he was referred to as the world champion, even though no one outside the Sierra Nevadas had heard of him.

Allen Hubbard from Portland witnessed the races at La Porte and through the *Lewiston* (Maine) *Journal* told Mainers about the races. "Here in New England you get plenty of exercise when you go skeeing in the fields and on the hills," wrote Hubbard, "but there's another side to the sport that you find only in the west.

"I heard much talk of skees the first fall I was in the Sierra country. Of skee riding; how to put on a good bottom; the proper dope for hot and dry snow; the proper length of the skee; and the advantages of spruce, pine and fir, for making them. I heard stories of the wonderful rides and phenomenal performances of some of the best riders. But always in the end, the talk drifted to the discussion of dope.

The starter, beside Frank Stewart with his ever-present dope box, is about to hit a circular saw blade to start a saw-off, or race.

"Traveling dope, racing dope, dope for cold snow, wet snow, dry snow and hot snow. To me it seemed strange that it should make any difference what one put on the bottom of a skee. Here in the east I had only been acquainted with the snowshoe.

"I learned it is really not the riding so much as the men who make the dope who win the skee races."

"Traveling

dope,

racing dope,

dope for

cold snow,

wet snow,

dry snow

and

hot snow."

Stewart never found much gold but he did achieve fame as the dean of the dope makers. "Frank wouldn't let anyone see him preparing his dopes," said his wife Alice. "He worked with his pots on the kitchen stove. I can still smell it brewing—balsam, camphor, paraffin, oil of hemlock—a good clean smell. He made large cakes of it and had different recipes for every kind of snow and weather."

The *La Porte Union* wrote, "The day before the races small squads of men were scattered all over the hill, testing the quality of their mixtures." Stewart was always there, directing and coaching his racers, with his box of dope held tightly in his hand.

Longboard races went straight down the mountain on 12' skis with only a leather toe loop holding the skier to the

ski. Turning these longboards was impossible—the first one to the bottom won. Speeds of 60 mph were common and the record was 88 mph.

"The start is exciting," wrote Hubbard. "Near the two start poles are the two judges. They sight along the poles. Each man must have his toes back of the line. As the race track is descending there is a man behind each racer to hold the skees till he starts. They used a big circular saw as a gong, the starter hit the saw and the racers start. Using their poles they push themselves over the ground then they drop down onto their haunches."

"I can still visualize the riders coming down the hill," said Alice Stewart. "They came so fast you could hardly see them at the finish."

The finish line was usually marked by a portable bar and there was heavy betting on the races. Hubbard wrote, "As the racers crossed the finish line all the crowd of men made a rush for the bar where drinks had been served through the afternoon; everyone ordered what they wanted and the winner settled the score. That is the unwritten law of the races, the winner pays for the drinks."

"The entire life of the community in the winter centered around snowshoeing and preparations for the winter races," said

Frank Stewart doping a pair of skis. He always carefully guarded his dope box.

Alice Stewart. "Everyone had a good time at the races, but as a young girl I didn't care much for that excitement. It was the dances every night after the races that I liked the best. It was there that I met Frank. He was dark and handsome and had a beard that reached his chest. I was 18 and Frank was 44. It was a romance of the ski trail I guess."

After his career as a racer Stewart made racing skis, dope and coached a stable of racers. In a career spanning six decades Stewart and his racers were consistent winners. In March, 1911 at what ended up being the all-time finale of longboard racing in the Sierras, one of Stewart's top racers switched from his Old Black Dope to a dope made by a rival. The defection hurt Stewart's feelings and that night he drank, something he was never known to do. Late that night he said that the next day's races would be his last. Racing for Stewart and using Old Black Dope, Jim Mullen skied the 1500' slope in 14 seconds to win. That is an average speed of 73 mph, from a standing start.

Despite the victory, Stewart kept his pledge and retired. He gave away his longboards and shared some of his dope recipes.

Thus a Mainer from Skowhegan not only found fame in the snow covered gold mining camps of California as the top dope maker of his time—he also won the fair maiden.

THE SKI-ING GIRL

RECIPE

After his retirement in 1911 Stewart shared the recipe for Old Black Dope, one of his most famous for cold hard snow. He won races with Old Black Dope from 1869 until he retired. Stewart kept the cooking time secret.

- *2 oz. spermaceti (whale oil)*
- *1/4 oz. pine pitch*
- *1/8 oz. camphor*
- *1 tablespoon balsam fir*
- *1 tablespoon oil of spruce.*

Ski-Spree

WHEN P-TEX SKI BASES BECAME POPULAR IN THE 1950'S PERFORMANCE MINDED SKIERS HAD A PROBLEM. EXISTING WAXES WERE FAST BUT THEY DID NOT ADHERE WELL TO THE NEW BASES. RAY LETARTE FROM GORHAM EXPERIMENTED UNTIL HE CAME UP WITH A FAST AND LONG LASTING WAX WHICH HE MARKETED AS SKI-SPREE. EACH FALL LETARTE MELTED HIS UNIQUE WAX RECIPE, A COMBINATION OF A SPECIALLY FORMU-LATED BRONZE POWDER, ACID AND CERACIN (INSTEAD OF PARAFIN). HE POURED THE MIXTURE INTO CUPCAKE TINS TO HARDEN. FOR DAYS EVERY NOOK AND CRANNY IN THE LETARTE HOUSEHOLD WAS TAKEN UP WITH CUPCAKE TINS OF HARDENING WAX.

THE UNUSUALLY SHAPED WAX, WITH ITS DISTINCTIVE BRONZE COLOR, WORKED BEST ON WET SPRING SNOW AND WAS POPULAR INTO THE 1970S.

THE WARDEN IS COMING

"When people saw my ski tracks

in the woods it was as if a

loud speaker had announced

over the countryside,

The Warden Is Coming."

"My father

asked me, 'How would you like to go to America,'" Frederick Jorgensen wrote in his autobiography. "The question was indeed a bolt from the blue, but I seemed to be getting in too much trouble in Sweden so I said 'Sure' before I had given it a second thought." In 1882 Jorgensen followed his countrymen to New Sweden, Maine. Jorgensen worked at a variety of jobs. In 1902 he supervised a ditch digging crew for the Fish and Game Commission. Once again he found himself in trouble.

25 YEARS A GAME WARDEN

Frederick Jorgensen

"THE

GENTLEMAN

CALLED ME NAMES,

SO I USED ONE OF

MY MILITARY

SCHOOL HOLDS

ON HIM, A GOOD

SNOR-TWISTER,

UNTIL THE MAN

YELLED LIKE A

LOON AND KICKED

UP AND DOWN

LIKE A HORSE

WITH SPAVIN."

"The gentleman called me names, so I used one of my Military School holds on him, a good snor-twister, until the man yelled like a loon and kicked up and down like a horse with spavin. The rest of the gang came to his assistance, so I let him go with a push and the poor fellow sat down massaging his dislocated nose. I warded off the rest who started to set upon me by using a birch stick which I wielded like a sabre."

The Fish and Game Commission heard about Jorgensen's feisty spirit and hoped he could help solve a problem. Poaching was very common. "Sportsmen" slaughtered dozens of deer or moose and some lumber camps ate large quantities of illegal venison. Poachers didn't appreciate game wardens trying to stop them so they threatened the wardens and scared them off.

The head of the Fish and Game Commission said to Jorgensen, "I want to send them a good man, one not only physically fit but someone with courage. After last night I'm satisfied you will fit the bill."

"My first day there was a Sunday and a glorious one at that," wrote Jorgensen. "There wasn't a single cloud on the horizon nor a breath of wind in the air. Overhead birds of all kinds flew around in great flocks. I couldn't help myself, but shouted, 'Glory Hallelujah.' I thought to myself it was so beautiful I'd rather be in the Maine woods than in the best city in the world.

"There was a time when the game warden was not only unpopular but pretty generally avoided. Before I went into the warden service in 1902 I was warned that I wouldn't be popular. The warning was proved one time when I returned to camp and found a stick of dynamite in the ashes waiting for me to restart my fire.

"No one around Wilson Mills used skis when I was there and most of them had never seen any. When mine arrived, they caused a great sensation. There was a crowd assembled at the hotel and the skis came in for a great deal of ridicule. We argued the merits of snowshoes versus skis in deep snow, so I suggested 'Let's settle it right now. I'll race your best snowshoer to the Post Office and back, the first one back gets one of Mrs. Flint's fresh mince pies'. Well we started our half mile race and by the time the poor fellow reached the Post Office I was nearly back to the Hotel."

One spring Jorgensen made a trip on

skis to lumber camps looking for signs of poaching. "The morning was warm and the skiing hard on account of the snow that stuck to my skis," he wrote. "I did not have a kit of ten waxes that I hear skiers of today carry. After five miles I came upon bear tracks. As every hunter knows, the lure of unusual tracks in the woods is irresistible, so I swung my skis around and followed them. Suddenly I heard a rending howl, too close for comfort. The snow was loose in the protected valley and I knew I could out-run the bear downhill on my skis. I pulled my revolver in case of emergency and took a good look to see what the bear's intentions were. She raised herself, with a baby bear between her fore-paws. She threw it up a spruce tree, gave a grunt and the little thing climbed up until it reached a limb. She did it with a second cub, who didn't like the idea of climbing a tree, but the mother bear cuffed it and up the tree it went.

"The mother bear turned toward me and gave one unholy roar. She didn't need to worry, because I couldn't have shot her anymore than a human being. She was a mother protecting her children. Probably some lumberjack frightened her away from her winter quarters to a safer place.

"When people saw my ski tracks in the woods it was as if a loud speaker had announced over the countryside, The Warden Is Coming." Jorgensen sometimes hid his skis and used snowshoes just so he could move around without leaving his signature tracks behind.

Jorgensen served notice to poachers, he was on the job and was fast enough to catch them. "I didn't have a college educa-tion so I had to use my brain," he wrote. Jorgensen served as a game warden for 25 years. He convinced many people of the importance of protecting fish and game of the Maine woods and stopped the unchecked poaching. Jorgensen wrote, "I have seen the forces of conservation increase and seen the Department of Inland Fisheries and Game develop into an organi-zation fitting the require-ments of modern times."

"Time and again I have regretted my boy-ish foolishness, but I have never regretted the fact that I came to Maine."

JORGENSEN SOMETIMES HID
S SKIS AND USED SNOWSHOES
O HE COULD MOVE AROUND
WITHOUT LEAVING HIS
SIGNATURE TRACKS BEHIND.

America's First Ski Book

A PORTLAND CITIZEN, 48-YEAR-OLD

CABINETMAKER AND SHIPWRIGHT

THEODORE JOHNSEN WAS ABOUT TO

MAKE HISTORY IN 1905 — BY WRITING

THE FIRST AMERICAN SKI BOOK.

The front pages

of the Portland, Maine newspapers of December 1905 were filled with details of the big snow storm that had just come up the Atlantic coast. The storm put an end to the automobile season for the year. The sports pages reported the six-day bicycle race in Madison Square Garden. Baseball and football got lots of space. There was even a report that basketball might be played indoors that winter. But there was nothing about skiing.

Skiing was a rare sport in the Northeast. Except in a few towns settled heavily by Scandinavians such as New Sweden, Maine, and Berlin, New Hampshire, skiing was hardly known. Yet one of Portland's citizens, a 48-year-old cabinetmaker and shipwright named Theodore A. Johnsen was about to make history in 1905—by writing the first American ski book.

Johnsen immigrated from Manchester, England, as a 21-year-old to work with his father, a cabinetmaker who had come to Maine earlier. The two worked together constructing and carving pews for Portland's Lutheran Church.

Possibly as a result, Johnsen married a Lutheran churchgoer, Hilda Ek who had immigrated from Sweden. The couple took an active part in Portland's Swedish community church activities. So far, nothing unusual. But when Johnsen was in his late 30s, he left the beaten path.

Inspired by an article in the April, 1895 issue of *Scientific American* Johnsen began to ski with help from Swedish friends. He probably made his own skis, although he could have bought them from such manufacturers as Martin Strand who had been making skis for ten years. Or he could have bought skis from the Johnston Hardware Co. of Bangor, Maine, which had printed in 1903 what may have been the first American ski catalog, advising that it sold "the finest skis of solid native ash, complete with leather harness for $2.95." Or Johnsen could have bought them from Lars Stadig of New Sweden, Maine, who made skis for sale.

"SKEEING IS A GLORIOUS SPORT. IT NEVER GROWS TAME OR UNINTERESTING,

THE EXHILARATING JOY OF IT IS A DELIGHT BEYOND ALL COMPARISON."

During the time he was rising steadily in his trade, skiing was only a recreation as far as Johnsen was concerned. In 1900 Johnsen was made foreman of a boat-building company in Portland.

engine was bulky and took too much room. A 1905 article in *Outing Magazine* titled "The Motor Boat Of The Future," said, "Unless all signs fail, the typical pleasure craft of the not distant future will be the so called 'gasoline cruiser'. It is a type of vessel so new that the public at large may be said to be entirely ignorant of its existence." Showing the resemblance to another gasoline powered novelty the article went on, "The automobile cruiser will cost perhaps a trifle less than a steam yacht of the same size."

Johnsen recognized this fundamental change in boating and Tajco made two boat designs. Both were about 30 feet long and were gasoline powered pleasure crafts. They slept two and had a bathroom on board. These boats were for the wealthy who could afford an expensive boat of this type.

Johnsen's ad in the 1905 *Maine Register* read "Speciality—Power Cruisers," and then almost as an afterthought, "Also Manufacturers of Norwegian skiis and Indian Snow Shoes." (This is the only time he didn't spell it skees.)

Tajco's earliest surviving business records date back to February, 1905. They show that Johnsen was

THE WINTER SPORT OF SKEEING

AS DEAR TO

JOHNSEN'S

HEART AS THEY

WERE TO ANY OF

THE EARLY SKI

PIONEERS.

In 1904 Johnsen saw a fundamental change in boating about to take place and started his own boat-building and wood products company, the Theo A. Johnsen Co, also known as Tajco.

Most of the boats on the Maine coast, both working and pleasure boats, were sailing vessels. There were commercial steamships and some wealthy people had steam driven pleasure craft, but the steam selling a "Telemark" and a "Regulation Skee" as well as snowshoes, wood novelties and the Portland Ash Sifter on which he had imprinted, "It will save 1/4 of the coal."

Johnsen must have been encouraged by the sales of his skis that first winter of 1904-05 because in May, he began to invest seriously in marketing an expanded line of skis for the coming 1905-06 season. His emphasis shifted away from the "automobile cruiser" to winter sports and skiing in particular. His efforts included traveling salesmen who sold many of his Portland Ash Sifters and skis.

As part of this effort, he laid out and printed a ski booklet 54 pages long, entitled *The Winter Sport Of Skeeing*. The first 38 pages was an instruction manual in technique and in the use of equipment. The last 16 pages consisted of the Tajco 1905 winter sports catalog. (The catalog was also printed separately). This booklet constitutes the first substantive work on skiing published in America. It was available for 10 cents, postpaid.

The fact that the first American ski book was written by a rank amateur whose main occupation was cabinetmaker and boat builder is astounding. Johnsen's little volume was one of the first ever published in English on the sport.

The first book had been co-authored only the year before by an intrepid ski pioneer named E.C. Richardson. *Ski-Running* was published in London in 1904. Richardson was one of a handful of Englishmen who had learned to ski in Norway, where the sport was far advanced

THE WINTER SPORT OF SKEEING

"In open country where the wind has a good chance to sweep skee sailing offers a sport which comes very close to actual flying," wrote Theo Johnsen.

Norjalainen Suksi

On Valloittanut Amerikan

Hiihtäminen on kaikkein vilkkain urheiluista talviseen aikaan sekä yhdelle ja kahdelle henkilölle että kokonaisille seuruoille; antaa helpon kulkuneuvon missä vain on lunta ja on halpaa iloa ihmisille joka ikää.

Meillä on mainioita ja oivalhsia THEO. A. JOHNSEN Co: nin "TAJCO" suksia; olemme tilaisuudessa myymään mitä parhaimpia suksia, jokaista vaadittua mittaa, halvoilla hinnoilla.

Like many of Johnsen's ads this one is in Finnish

over that practiced anywhere else in the world. Richardson had extracted hard-won knowledge through apprenticeship with acknowledged masters in the historic homeland of the sport.

Johnsen was not deterred by his own relative inexperience. In typically American fashion, he got around his lack of European travel and his limited store of experience simply by borrowing from abroad. Some of his artwork is quite obviously copied from Richardson's book and he lifted part of his technical discussion directly from Richardson as well.

Even so, there is no question that skiing's sensations and beauty were as dear to Johnsen's heart as they were to any of the early ski pioneers. None but a true lover of the sport could have composed the praise heaped on the sport in his booklet.

"Skeeing," he wrote, "is indeed a glorious sport. It never grows tame or uninteresting, the exhilarating joy of it is a delight beyond all comparison.

"The introduction of modern, lightweight skees has made it possible for all ages and both sexes to enjoy traveling over snow-clad land breathing in the clear, crisp air and feasting the eyes on the passing landscape and its myriad panoramic charms. What supreme delights the skee runner finds in noting the vagaries of landscape as he glides along!

"Snow itself is capable of many wonderful changes, including downy, fluffy, powdery, sandy, dusty, flowery, crystalline, brittle, gelatinous, salt-like, slithery and watery forms. Snow will be found as hard and white as marble, other times the skidor will find a layer of soft powdery snow over a hard surface.

"The delight of gliding rather than tramping over the snow-clad surface has been called the 'poetry of skee progress'. As the experienced skidor dashes down the crusted hillsides with the speed of the wind there comes to the sport an exhilertion and excitement that positively knows no equal. Any skidor will tell you that skeeing is the most fascinating, most healthful and most delightful of all winter sports and that it is indeed an ideal outdoor pastime for young and old."

Johnsen prepared an advertising campaign for "Skeeing - America's greatest winter sport" and for Tajco skees. He placed ads in national publications as well as local newspapers. He ran ads in *Youths Companion, National Sportsman* and in *Canoeing* magazine. Appealing to the better educated and the wealthy, Johnsen even advertised in *McClures*, a literary journal. The ads he ran were general in nature, extolling the fun and the health benefits of skiing. One ad he used frequently said, "The ideal winter pastime for both sexes and all ages. The happiest, healthiest hours of winter will be those spent on Tajco skees."

Johnsen held a joint marketing campaign with *National Sportsman*. Readers were asked to help get subscribers for *National Sportsman* and would be paid with either cash or Tajco skees.

In the fall of 1905, Johnsen seemed confident that, given the opportunity to buy proper equipment and told how to go about it, large numbers of people would take to skiing. Johnsen backed his confidence with effort and by December, he had 31 people working for him in an ambitious winter sporting goods manufacturing and distributing operation.

Johnsen used his inventiveness to solve the ongoing disagreement as to whether a skier should use one pole or two by offering a combination Push Stick. This model could be used as two separate poles as the Scandinavians did on flat terrain. When skiers came to a downhill section, they could lock the poles together and use them as one pole.

Tajco offered 12 models of skis beginning at $3.50 and going as high as $18.00. (Others sold mostly cheap equipment. In his December, 1905 advertisements, in the *Portland Sunday Telegram*, M. Mckechnie of Sherbrooke, Quebec sold his 9 foot "Gents model for $3.75 which "includes the guiding stick.")

Johnsen sent skis on consignment to hardware stores and general stores all over New England (at the time, there were no ski shops as such). Through the end of 1905, Johnsen delivered 506 pairs of lowest price ski. The next three most popular models were priced at $7.00 and he delivered about 170 pairs of each, a total of over 1,000 skis.

In January, 1906, Johnsen met his first setback. Many of the consigned skis were returned unsold.

Johnsen's main competitor, Martin Strand, was also familiar with the problem of price resistance. Strand began making

skis in 1896 in Minneapolis and was probably the only other major commercial ski manufacturer in the U.S. In the 1931 book *History of the National Ski Association and the Ski Sport*, Strand wrote, "When I started I soon learned that I could make more skis than I could sell, for I had no selling plan nor any selling experience."

Johnsen re-organized his sales approach. He no longer sent skis on consignment and relied more on his three representatives who traveled as far as Salt Lake City equipped with exquisite scale models of each ski. Stores bought the models and used them to sell the skis. The catalog reassured the potential buyer that skis would be "worked absolutely true to the model."

Most of Tajco's pre-season sales went to heavily-Scandinavian Midwestern cities. Often when Johnsen's salesmen went to a store which had bought skis the previous year they found the skis still there, unsold.

Johnsen manufactured too many expensive, high-quality skis which remained unsold. By November, 1906 he was selling his equipment at substantially reduced prices to anyone who would buy in quantity. His passion for skiing was so great he had believed people sharing his passion would begin buying the best. Johnsen was wrong. In the days when the winter outdoors was mostly shunned by adults, Johnsen had a vision of America on good, sturdy, well-made skis, but the American public was not ready for Theodore Johnsen's vision.

Strand was more realistic. In a letter written to a customer in 1914, Strand wrote "The average young American is a sort of hot house plant, who does not care to spend much time out of doors, as the cheap show houses and pool rooms seem to be more attractive. They do not want to spend enough money on a pair of skis so that cheap skis are the only ones that have sold in any quantity in this country up to the present time."

The final entries in the business records of the Theodore A. Johnsen Company came in February, 1907. Shortly thereafter, Johnsen closed Tajco and moved to Massachusetts.

Johnsen still had a lot of inventory left. He sold what inventory he could, even unfinished equipment. This must have been hard for a man who took as much pride in his design and workmanship as Johnsen did.

The *Somerville* (Mass.) *Journal* for November 1, 1911, recorded that "Theodore A. Johnsen died suddenly from kidney trouble at the Boston City Hospital Monday afternoon. He was suddenly stricken fatally that morning at a Boston factory where he was employed as a wood-carver. His health had been failing for two years." Johnsen was 54.

Theo A. Johnsen recognized fundamental changes about to happen in two sports yet was unable to capitalize on either one. But he had left a bequest to the sport of skiing—America's first ski book, a testimonial matched in fervor by few skiers since.

In the studio: All of the equipment photos in *The Winter Sport Of Skeeing* were shot in a studio in Portland. This photo showing the bindings in use was retouched to remove the carpet and the elaborate, wheeled backdrop.

The Carnival Craze

FRIDAY NIGHT THE KING AND QUEEN OF

THE CARNIVAL LED A TORCHLIGHT

PARADE FROM MONUMENT SQUARE TO

THE NOVELTY OF AN OUTDOOR PARTY

UNDER THOUSANDS OF INCANDESCENT

LIGHTS AT DEERING OAKS PARK.

Daring Jumpers Shoot Into Space

Skiing was still confined mainly to Maine's Scandinavian communities. By 1916, the summer resort at Poland Spring began to stay open for winter sports enthusiasts, offering cross-country skiing and ski jumping lessons. About the same time, the Bethel Inn began offering winter sports to guests: it had a 1/3 mile long toboggan run starting on top of a raised wooden chute, an ice skating pond and trail maps for "Snowshoe Trails"used by both snowshoers and skiers.

In the 1920s Maine cities and towns began to hold winter carnivals. Portland and Augusta vied with each other to stage the most elaborate carnivals. Augusta built an electric windmill to house their jump tower and invited Governor Percival Baxter to open the festivities. Portland attracted some of the East's best jumpers for its carnivals.

The 1924 winter carnival in Portland was perhaps that city's biggest and best carnival. "Guests Arrive For Portland Winter Carnival, Opening Today," read the banner

Cars lined Saint John St. and over 5,000 spectators watched the jumpers on Portland's Western Promenade ski jump.

headline across the top of the *Portland Press Herald* in February, 1924. A photo dominated the front page captioned, "King and Queen Of The Portland Winter Carnival, And Their Court". Crowded into one column with a small headline was a story about the tribute being paid to President Woodrow Wilson who had just died.

The King and Queen of the 1924 Portland Winter Carnival with two pages carrying the Queen's train.

THE QUEEN

WORE A JEWELED

DRESS OF PALE

PINK SATIN AND

THE KING HAD AN

ELABORATE SUIT

OF BRIGHT RED.

BOTH WORE

ROYAL PURPLE

ROBES TRIMMED

WITH ERMINE.

Hey, this was the Roaring 20s. Party On! "Coronation Ceremony is the climax to the first day of the carnival," wrote the Portland Press Herald. "Leading the coronation procession were four princesses of royal blood, followed by two pages bearing on cushions the crowns of the King and Queen, next came the royal couple. The Queen, Miss Winona Drew, wore a jeweled dress of pale pink satin and a robe of royal purple trimmed with ermine and the King, Major E. E. Philbrook, had an elaborate suit of bright red with a royal purple robe trimmed with ermine. The radiantly beauti-ful first lady of the Carnival lightly rested her hand on the arm of the stalwart monarch of the Carnival realm. Following the royal pair were two pages holding the Queen's train.

"The archbishop came onto the stage with two heralds and impressively placed the coronets on the heads of the King and Queen, vesting them with authority to rule over the realm of Portland until the close of the Carnival on Saturday night."

Three teams of Eskimo sled dogs provided one of the highlights of the carnival. Veterans of several Arctic expeditions, they ran a 25 mile race through the city streets.

On Friday, however, their mission was uncharacteristic. "This morning the Queen is to make a shopping tour with the Whitehouse dog team," wrote the Portland Press Herald. "She will be dressed in her imported white wool outdoor costume which was picked out for her at the New York fashion show. Her arctic limousine with its wealth of fur robes standing in front of a Congress Street store will be evidence that the First Lady Of The Realm is inside doing her carnival shopping."

Friday's events also included skating and cross-country races and horse racing on the ice-covered track of the Deering Oaks Speedway. "The spectators who lined the frozen track were given an unexpected

THE MAINE HISTORICAL SOCIETY COLLECTIONS

bit of excitement when Carl C, close on the flying heels of Robert M and Gold Quartz, fell to the ice and slid 25 feet on his sweat-covered flank. Neither the horse nor the driver was injured.

"While the heats on the speedway were in progress, the cross-country ski race started. Ten contestants, with skis laced firmly to their feet for the six mile grind, got away at a pace that only athletes trained in the use of the long sticks can stand."

Saturday was the busiest day of the carnival, beginning with the dog sled race. Other events included a variety of 50, 100 and 220 yard dashes on skis and snow-shoes. In one 50 yard dash contestants wore one ski and one snow-shoe. A snowshoe dash was run blindfolded. An obstacle race was run for kids, who had to crawl through barrels while wearing skis.

Before the ski jumping event, Birger Olsen, a well-known jumper and president of the Portland Ski Club, said, "The sugary snow that fell recently has made the jump exceptionally fast and some long jumps should be made by the contestants."

Olsen was arguably Portland's best known athlete, a champion jumper who had won competitions in Sweden, Norway and Canada. Now, at age 45, he was still a fine jumper. A year earlier three members of his family had come from Berlin, New Hampshire, to compete in Portland's carnival. Sixty-year old Olaf Olsen jumped despite several bad falls. Eleven-year old Clarence Olsen jumped so well he was awarded a special cup. Christine Olsen won the women's 50 yard snowshoe race. Birger himself jumped well but fell on the hard snow and severely bruised his side.

Birger wanted to redeem himself.

"Smiling his favor on Portland's three day carnival in his honor, King Winter attended Saturday's events with his bright-eyed, red-cheeked associates, Sunny Skies and Bracing Air," wrote the *Portland Press Herald.*

"When a crowd of over 5,000 people gather in one locality to witness an event, something must be

The PARIS SKI

A Paris Manufacturing catalog from the 1920s

THE MAINE HISTORICAL SOCIETY COLLECTIONS

The Portland Winter Carnival Committee hired Birger Olsen, working as a carpenter, to build a ski jump. They later discovered he was a champion ski jumper.

going on. That's how it was at the Western Promenade when ski jumpers of international fame lifted howling masses of humans into the heights of excitement and ecstasy. Shooting down the smooth takeoff like rockets, the daring jumpers shot into space far above the heads of the spectators who lined the bottom of the slope just off St. John Street and ended their wild flight way beyond the car tracks, or frequently, in a flying tangle of arms, legs and skis at the bottom of the steep incline. While this nerve-wracking contest was on another sensation appeared when the winning sled dog team driven by Harold Whitehouse of Boothbay Harbor ended the 25 mile derby at the foot of the Promenade in the thick of the crowd."

The King and Queen prepare to take their "arctic limousine" from Portland's West End to Congress St. to shop.

THE MAINE HISTORICAL SOCIETY COLLECTIONS

The first jumper was 15 year old Miss Margaret Towne from Berlin, New Hampshire. Margaret was a good jumper and being female was a bit of a novelty. She jumped the year before and had been admired for her "brilliant landings and her unsurpassed courage." Not able to actually enter the competition, she jumped in each round as an exhibition.

"The police and carnival officials were hard pressed to keep the eager crowds back of the lines. Ropes from the top of the hill to the bottom along the sides of the ski course were under constant strain from the pressure of the masses, and once a score of spectators, mostly youngsters, were spilled in a veritable tin soldier heap as the rope to which they were clinging gave way. They all piled up together at the bottom of the steep incline and no one was the worst for wear, although it took a lot of untangling before everyone was able to stand on their feet.

"Miss Margaret Towne, a winsome lass of 15, clad in an all white woolen sport suit, electrified the crowd thrice with excellent jumps off the high runway. Remembering her from the previous year people cheered her with vim as she sailed

Jumpers frequently landed in a "flying tangle of arms, legs and skis at the bottom of the steep incline".

THE MAINE HISTORICAL SOCIETY COLLECTIONS

Tubbs Catalog from the 1920's

on her swift flight through space.

"Also winning the instant support of the throng was a boy, a mere 'kid,' Clarence Olsen. He jumped with the best of them and while unable to place with the experts for distance he showed extraordinary form and kept his feet better than most of his elders on the snowpath."

The first two jumps were scored on a combination of form and distance. The third was for the longest standing jump.

Top jumpers such as Erling Anderson, Ernest Pederson and Dewey Couture, the previous year's winner with a hill record of 84', were all looking to win the distance jump. In the third round 61 year old Olaf Olsen set the pace with a jump of 82' 4". Ernest Pederson, who won the first portion of the competition, jumped 84' 1", barely setting a new hill record. Erling Anderson immediately broke it by going 92' 2". The next day Birger Olsen's picture was on the front page of the paper, but the headline read, "Olsen Jumps 92' 6" But Falls When Landing." He finished fourth overall in the competition.

Birger Olsen jumped high and far but fell on the landing.

"Portland's third and most magnificent carnival will not shortly pass from memory," continued the *Portland Press Herald*. "The joyous spirit of the multitude of red blooded manhood and womanhood that stirred and thrilled them with skill and daring will not soon be lost. There will be other carnivals but Portland has reached the height of splendid accomplishment in its winter sports festivals."

Playing In The Great Snow Empire

PHOTOS COURTESY OF: FORT FAIRFIELD PUBLIC LIBRARY

In 1936 and again in 1937 a four day race was run from Bangor to Caribou, a distance of 180 miles. Unfortunately the weather did not cooperate for either race; racers had to contend with rain while they skied roads that had been plowed and sanded. Bob Johnson, the winner of the 1936 race, wore out two pair of wooden skis before winning on his third pair.

In 1937 the town of Fort Fairfield staged the Tri-Town Marathon. The race was laid out from Fort Fairfield to Caribou, to Presque Isle and back to Fort Fairfield. Racers covered 35 miles a day and repeated the loop three consecutive days. The Tri-Town Marathon attracted some of the best ski marathoners in Maine.

Eighteen skiers started the Tri-Town race but only eight finished. Of those eight three were from New Sweden. *The Bangor Daily News* wrote, "In New Sweden ski artistry is taught as one of the fundamentals of healthy living and as one of the finest recreational pursuits that a man can follow. From childhood and up people in New Sweden claim the land of snow for their own, beating a merry tune with their ski runners along unbroken trails and a speedy downhill run. Both young and old revel in the zestful sport." (Even today when you talk with someone from New Sweden about skiing you are talking about cross-country not downhill skiing.)

People came from all over to participate and watch the carnival. "Snow trains from Maine's cities and towns and special railroad fares from Boston and other points will afford winter sports fans an opportunity of participating in the Fort Fairfield Winter Carnival which is considered to be one of the leading events of its kind to be held in the eastern U.S," wrote the *Bangor Daily News*. A round trip ticket from Bangor on the "Aroostook Flyer" was $2.50.

The ski marathon was not the only test of endurance. "The skating marathon is also listed as a three day event with two-man teams skating one and one half hours each day," wrote the *Bangor Daily News*.

"The greatest number of laps covered during the event will determine the winner." Snow was cleared from the Aroostook River to create a race track for the horses. Ice racing attracted many of New England's best trotters and pacers. Other events included ski-joring, ski jumping, hockey, snowshoe races, dog races, wood chopping and a girls' ski potato race. (This is, after all, Aroostook County.)

"The 1937 Fort Fairfield winter carnival was probably the best of the carnivals," recalls Alden Anderson from New Sweden. "They had the most ski events. There was jumping, cross-country for the kids, ski obstacle races, a slalom race and of course the Tri-Town Marathon."

"Despite a mercury that hovered at 30 below zero gaily costumed disciples of King Winter thronged this Carnival spirited town to watch the start of the race," wrote the *Bangor Daily News*.

"It was kinda cold that morning," says Alden Anderson. "We left about eight in the morning and it was 30 below. Boy, that's cool to get out there and get going. Some of us wore white uniforms that were from the New Sweden Athletic Club. On that first day we wrapped newspapers around ourselves, under our uniforms, to cut the wind."

"Roads were plowed then so we skied on the very side," recalls Harold Bondeson.

"There was a bit of snow we could ski on.

"A station wagon followed us in case we needed some water or something to eat. If some guy dropped out they picked him up.

"That 1937 Tri-Town race was one of the very best races for everyone to look at. Cars followed us around the course. State police cars escorted us to make sure we didn't have any trouble."

On the first day of the carnival, Laverne Anderson from New Sweden established a big lead in the marathon. Lela Dean, from Fort Fairfield, won the open ski competition, 100 yard obstacle race and finished her big day by also winning the girls' potato race. Clair Lockhart received attention by being the only girl to go off the big jump on Fisher Hill, and carried herself well with a 75' jump. In horse racing, the lightly regarded Hoyle beat the favorite trotter, Bonnie M, with one of the fastest heats ever made on the local ice track.

Prizes at the Fort Fairfield Carnival were some of the best of any carnival. Bass donated jumping boots, Walter Stadig donated skis and other merchants donated car radios, watches, poles and a variety of other merchandise. Prizes were on display in store windows. Competitors looked at the prizes and tried that much harder to win their event.

Before the start of the second day of racing Governor Barrows spoke to the car-

Detail of a bear trap binding from the 1930s

CHUB CLARK

Laverne Anderson racing on the side of the plowed road in the 1937 Tri-Town Marathon.

nival crowd. He outlined his hope for the future of Maine as a winter sports site.

The racers had a warmer day to race but it still wasn't easy. "One thing you run into on these long races is blisters," says Alden Anderson. "We had blisters on our hands and feet. You had a lot of blisters before you were done. At night we put iodine on them, wrapped them up and the next day we'd go again."

The racers used head high poles with no wrist straps. The grip was long so the racers could hold it low or high depending on how they were skiing. They wore woolen mittens with a leather cover. The lack of a wrist strap meant racers had to keep a tight grip on their poles and loose mittens contributed to the blister problem.

The Bangor Daily News wrote, "Later that day Roland Chasse and Basil White, both 15 and from Fort Fairfield, thrilled carnival fans when they took a dangerous sky ride as they jumped hand-in-hand from the Fort Fairfield jump through a paper covered hoop.

"Ten thousand carnival enthusiasts stormed the village during the final day's program of the town's greatest winter

carnival. Saturday broke fine and clear, an ideal day for play in the great snow empire. The disciples of King Winter came early and stayed late, jamming the Main Street and competitive sites with a gay mass of multi colored ski suits, worn by young and old."

The slalom race started on Fort Hill, came down through some trees and finished between buildings in town. Spectators lined the course on the hill, as well as the streets and filled fire escapes of the buildings.

The Bangor Daily News wrote, "John Davenport, Fort Fairfield axman, split the timber in three quick cuts to successfully defend his 1936 crown in the Farmers Wood-Chopping Contest.

"Thousands packed the main go of the village to see the windup of the carnival's most spectacular event, the Tri-Town ski grind. Laverne Anderson, lanky ski flyer

Sylvia Russell, Queen of the 1937 Fort Fairfield Winter Carnival

from the sloping hills of New Sweden, led a pressing group of endurance men into town to cop first place in the Tri-Town Ski Marathon. Anderson's arrival was greeted with round after round of applause for his arduous feat over the three days."

Alden Anderson led Laverne into town on that final lap; he also won the second day's race, but had given so much time to Laverne on the first day that he came in second. Laverne won $50 for winning the marathon and Alden won a car radio for his second place finish. "I had a car so I was pretty excited about that radio," recalls Alden.

The 1937 Fort Fairfield race was one of the last of the big ski marathons. "That was one of the first years they plowed the roads," says Harold Bondeson. "When the open roads came it changed the way of traveling and ski-ing became less common. It was difficult to ski on the paved, plowed roads."

Social Event of the Season

"AT THE WINTER CARNIVALS WE HAD THREE NIGHTS OF DANCING. FOR US IT WAS THE SOCIAL EVENT OF THE SEASON. THE DANCE WAS IN A BIG HALL DECORATED FROM THE TOP DOWN. THERE WERE THRONES FOR THE KING AND QUEEN. IT LOOKED BEAUTIFUL. ONE YEAR AN ORCHESTRA FROM BOSTON CAME UP. THEY WERE UNDER THE IMPRESSION THEY WERE GOING INTO THE NORTH WOODS AND THEY DRESSED ACCORDINGLY. OUR LADIES OF THE TOWN HAD SPENT A LOT OF TIME PUTTING THEIR DRESSES TOGETHER AND LOOKED QUITE ELEGANT. THE MEMBERS OF THE ORCHESTRA WERE SHOCKED THAT FIRST NIGHT WHEN THEY WORE CASUAL CLOTHES AND THE LADIES WORE GOWNS. THE ORCHESTRA FELT AND LOOKED UNDER DRESSED. THE NEXT DAY THE ORCHESTRA DID BUSINESS WITH OUR LOCAL MERCHANTS AND BOUGHT SUITS THAT WERE APPROPRIATE FOR THE OCCASION.

"WE ALWAYS GOT A GOOD LAUGH ABOUT THAT ORCHESTRA."

—NORMA DORCEY

Maine Snow Trains

"THE HOMEWARD TRIP OF THE EIGHT CAR

TRAIN WAS THE USUAL FUNFEST WITH

HEARTY IF NOT HARMONIOUS SINGING

AND A VARIETY OF ANTICS CONSPIRING

TO KEEP AWAKE THESE SLEEPY EYED

INDIVIDUALS WHO HAD RUN THEIR STORE

OF ENERGY DOWN TO THE LAST DROP."

By the end of the 1920s groundwork had been laid for Maine skiing. Winter carnivals introduced skiing to many people, some of whom became skiers. Advertisements for trains taking skiers to ski slopes appeared as early as 1928. The Bethel Inn, Fryeburg Tavern, Log Lodge in Lucerne, Poland Spring Resort and the Eastland Hotel in Portland all were served by ski trains coming from Boston or Portland, and all offered skiing to their winter guests. The Rumford Winter Carnival in 1928 drew many spectators and competitors from Lewiston and Auburn who rode a train chartered for the event.

The imminent boom in the growth of skiing was delayed when the Great Depression arrived. Leisure time and sport were not options for most people—for the next few years little recreational skiing was done.

In 1933 President Roosevelt formed the CCC (Civilian Conservation Corps) to help the country cope with the Depression. Crews of CCC workers built bridges, worked on flood control and cut ski trails. In Maine the CCC cut trails on Pleasant Mtn., Mt. Blue, Mt. Megunticook and on Bigelow Mtn. Ski clubs formed and began cutting trails on mountains around Maine.

By 1935 Mainers were ready to enjoy life again and skiing in Maine was ready to begin one of its most exciting periods.

Fryeburg in 1935 was like any American town, struggling to regain prosperity. The Kiwanis Club sparked an idea to boost the town's economy: offer winter sports on a large scale and mount a large promotional effort. Thus was born the Fryeburg Winter Sports Committee.

Several hand printed promotional flyers are preserved in the Fryeburg Historical Society: one has the Kiwanis emblem drawn on a snowball bigger than the person pushing it and proclaims, "A hearty welcome is awaiting you in Fryeburg."

Lead toys from the 1930's

The Winter Sports Committee had the foresight to include the whole town; they put out a flyer explaining to townspeople that there would be a Ski Train "To advertise to as many people as possible the natural beauties and resources of the town." The flyer ended with, "Get out on the ski trails, snowshoe trails and toboggan chutes on Sunday afternoon. The bigger the crowd, the more fun—and the more fun the more people we will get on the next snow train, and there will certainly be another one. The cooperation of every person in town is needed to make this, THE FIRST SNOW TRAIN IN MAINE, a success."

Portland merchants supported the snow train by placing posters in their store windows. Newspaper ads and articles added to the excitement. The first train from Portland to Fryeburg ran on Sunday, February 3, 1935, and was a huge success. The *Portland Press Herald* headline announced: "229 Persons Make the Trip From Portland to Fryeburg on Maine's first M.C.

[Maine Central] Snow Train." Several hundred others came from nearby towns to enjoy the day. Asa Pike III, who was 24 when he helped spearhead Fryeburg's winter sports efforts, was over 80 when he laughed and said, "That probably doubled our population at that time."

The Fryeburg snow train was not the first but it did have a big impact. The people of the Bangor & Aroostook Railroad saw the ads for the Fryeburg train and liked the idea. On Friday, February 1, they contacted people in Greenville: they wanted to bring a trainload of people to Greenville that Sunday. Not wishing to turn down the opportunity to show off their town and make a few dollars, the townspeople said they would be ready. Luckily there was a CCC camp in town. On Saturday 100 men from the camp helped the townspeople prepare. They shoveled snow off Shadow Pond for skating, built a toboggan chute and packed the ski slope. Because of the growing interest in skiing, the spur-of-the-moment train to Greenville was just as much a success as the more carefully planned Fryeburg train.

The *Bangor Daily News* wrote, "Men, women and children packed the Bangor & Aroostook Snow Train that rolled into this snow bound and sun drenched village on the lower lip of Moosehead Lake. The snow patrons were greeted by a large delegation of natives, a fourteen inch blanket of snow and a flood of golden sunshine. Immediately after leaving the train the crowd surged up the road to the crest of a lofty ridge overlooking Shadow Pond. Rising from the peak of the ridge a toboggan chute and ski jump of new yellow lumber rose under the boughs of the pine and spruce.

"The train patrons lost no time in swinging into action and in a short time the steep ridge was packed with people who watched with interest those whizzing down the ski slide and toboggan chutes. After a wild dash down the snow blanketed slope the skiers and coasters sped out onto the surface of Shadow Pond.

"The long ski trails moved under the shadow of Little Squaw Mountain and wound serpentine through the ermine mantled forest.

"Many brought their own lunches and ate in the woods but the majority flocked back into the village for dinner in the hotel and little restaurants. All eating places were packed most of the afternoon.

"THE LONG SKI

TRAILS MOVED

UNDER THE

SHADOW OF

LITTLE SQUAW

MOUNTAIN AND

WOUND

SERPENTINE

THROUGH THE

ERMINE MANTLED

FOREST."

"Some of the skiers didn't return until the first blush of the descending sun swept the western horizon."

The success of their snow train in 1935 had convinced the Fryeburg Winter Sports Committee to do even more in 1936. On Starks Hill, behind the train station, they cut two ski trails offering advanced skiing. On Jockey Cap, wooden toboggan chutes were built to replace the snow-banked ones used in 1935. And then, putting up $25 each, ten enterprising young men built Maine's first rope tow. The tow brought experts, novices, the curious and a lot of attention to Fryeburg.

It was Maine's only rope tow for a mere two weeks. People in Bridgton had been skiing on the golf course at Bridgton Highlands and skating on the lake at the bottom of the ski hill. Two weeks after the tow opened at Fryeburg, another was operating at Bridgton Highlands.

For many years a narrow gauge train (the tracks were only two feet apart) had run in Bridgton. After the Depression this tiny train was a novelty and attracted fans who wanted to see and ride this unusual train.

"New England's Most Unique Sports Train", said the ads. The sports committee said, "The intention is to make a ride on this strange little railroad as much a part of the day's fun as the winter sports program."

The committee also built a Swiss chalet on top of Pleasant mountain. "The view of the White Mountains from the chalet is as beautiful as any in the Old World and snowbound Highland Lake has been aptly compared to the lakes of Killarney," said the committee.

In 1936, the Maine Central R.R. Snow Train from Union Station to Fryeburg cost $1.50 round trip. The booklet available on the train, *Winter Sports in Fryeburg*, told where to go and what to do. Ski equipment, snowshoes and toboggans could be rented on the Sport Car. In Fryeburg, eight horsedrawn haywagons took passengers to Pine Hill, where the novice skiers went and to Jockey Cap, to ride the tow or the toboggan chute. Houses with window cards welcomed anyone who wanted to come in to get dry. At the end of the day a crowd of spectators would stand watching

Avon Hilton at Dundee Heights in Gorham

37

the expert skiers negotiate the S turns at the bottom of Starks Hill.

The allure was not just skiing. *Along the Snow Trail* captured a bit of the flavor of the time: "The homeward trip of the eight car train was the usual funfest with hearty if not harmonious singing and a variety of antics conspiring to keep awake these sleepy eyed individuals who had run their store of energy down to the last drop. Nearly everybody was uncomfortably damp, thanks to spills that had filled pockets and sleeves with more snow than a snow loader could move in a day, but nobody cared. There were even mild sunburns, which is a point to call to the attention of relatives now basking under the same sun on Florida beaches. Come to Maine for a January sun tan!"

The townspeople of Fryeburg picked skiing as a vehicle for winter tourism. Time proved that they were right, but skiing's very popularity spawned competition. Portland skiers had many options. Bridgton offered skiing and a rope tow. After the CCC had cut a trail from the summit, Pleasant Mountain offered challenging skiing.

Skiing on Jockey Cap in Fryeburg in 1935 was the subject of one of the earliest color photographs published by National Geographic.

BACK TO THE *Best* IN SKI GEAR

BASS SKI BOOTS

Honors go to Bass Ski Boots from champs and novices alike, from Sun Valley to Lake Placid! Everyone who seeks good ski-ways agrees — the expert design, superior workmanship, quality materials of Bass Boots guarantee perfect support, balance, and comfort.

Luckily, this season brings better news to those who've had to do without Bass Boots. They're being manufactured again (though naturally not yet in pre-war quantity) and your dealer is receiving a fair share. If he's temporarily out of stock, keep trying! For slope conditions* are bound to be right when you wear Bass Ski Boots.

*And *after*-skiing conditions are swell when you wear hand-sewn Bass WEEJUNS — the all-time comfort shoe!

G. H. BASS & COMPANY
712 S. Main Street, Wilton, Maine

Bass Ski Boots

Portland skiers could join the Hockamock Ski Club which had a shelter and trails on Ossipee Mountain in Waterboro. They could join the Portland Ski Club which chartered a bus to take skiers to Douglas Mountain in Sebago. Many stayed right in Portland to ski on the fields at Stroudwater with the Deering High School skiers or on the golf course at Riverside.

On January 14, 1936, a charter bus advertisement appeared in *Along The Snow Trail:* "Ski Next Sunday At Ossipee Mountain – Only $1". This was 50¢ less than the train to Fryeburg. The following Tuesday an ad for the Fryeburg ski train read: "A Bargain 98¢ - a days fun at markdown prices. Up and back in a comfortable train for less than a dollar." The ski industry was getting competitive.

"The winter of 1937 wasn't a snowless winter, but it was darn close to it. And 1938 wasn't much better," recalls Avon Hilton, a long time Maine skier. The U.S. Weather Service in Portland shows the second lowest snowfall in the 113 years of keeping records: a paltry 29.4 inches of snow,

compared with 78.2 in the preceding winter and an average of 71.6 inches through the years. Snow trains didn't run from Portland to Fryeburg in 1937.

In 1938 Harvey Dow Gibson, a wealthy financier, purchased Cranmore Mountain in North Conway, New Hampshire, within 100 miles of Portland. With its sit-down lift, big mountain trails and the famous St. Anton ski instructor Benno Rybizka to head the ski school, Cranmore proved to be formidable competition.

In 1993 Asa Pike III recalled, "We were put out of business by ski slopes that were really ski slopes. There was no comparison between what we were doing and what Harvey Dow Gibson did in North Conway."

Ski areas, such as Bridgton Highlands which had opened on small hills were great to learn on, but once people learned to ski they wanted to go to a bigger hill. Bridgton moved its tow from the small hill at the Highlands to the open slope at the bottom of the racing trail at Pleasant Mountain. The tow and the racing trail proved to be so successful, the ski area on Pleasant Mountain is still open.

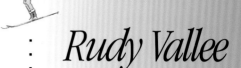

Rudy Vallee

RUDY VALLEE GREW UP IN WESTBROOK AND BEGAN HIS SHOW BIZ CAREER AT THE GEM THEATER ON PEAKS ISLAND IN CASCO BAY. IN A LETTER TO THE MAINE WINTER SPORTS FEDERATION, IN 1937, HE WROTE, "MAINE IS ALREADY A WORLD-BEATER AS FAR AS SUMMER SPORTS GO. THERE IS NO EARTHLY REASON WHY SHE CAN'T COMMAND RESPECT IN REGARD TO WINTER SPORTS.

"WHEN I WAS A KID WE WENT IN FOR BOBSLEDS, SNOWSHOEING AND IF SOME KID'S PARENT BOUGHT HIM A TOBOGGAN WE HELPED HIM WEAR IT OUT. WE DID A LITTLE SKIING - BUT IT'S ALL DIFFERENT TODAY.

"WHY NOT WORK OUT SOME DEAL WITH THE RAILROADS ON A WEEKEND SNOW TRAIN? I MEAN A DELUXE JOB WITH WEEKEND HOTEL PRIVELEGES, MEALS AND ENTERTAIN-MENT AND SKI INSTRUCTORS TO HELP."

A Chronology Of Maine Skiing

Theo A. Johnsen publishes the first book on skiing in the United States.

Maine's first skiers, hardy Swedish immigrants, settle New Sweden in Aroostook County.
1870

Frederick Jorgensen becomes a Maine game warden and uses skis to catch poachers.
1902

Paris Manufacturing begins selling moderately priced skis.
1905

Poland Spring Resort opens for skiers, offering lessons in cross country and jumping.
1916

1895
Theo A. Johnsen reads a *Scientific American* article on skiing, and takes up this new sport.

1904
In Portland, Theo A. Johnsen follows his passion and begins making high-quality Tajco ski equipment.

1907
Ahead of his time, Theo A. Johnsen faces stark reality and closes Tajco.

1921
Portland holds its first winter carnival, with regal pomp and wildly enthusiastic multitudes.

Rope and a pole-mounted rope tow gripper

Rumford holds its first winter carnival and draws thousands of spectators to this winter sports loving town.

Augusta builds an electrically powered windmill to house the inrun for its ski jump.
1923

Paris Manufacturing advertises, "A thoroughly high-grade ski that will satisfy the demands of the expert." The eight foot model sold for $7.20 and poles were $.90.

Bass sells a "Men's water-proofed Ski Shoe with a Plain Toe, Hard Box, Ski Heel and Norse Last."

Fort Fairfield holds its first winter carnival, a winter sports meet between three local high schools.
1927

Maine Central Railroad runs its first ski train from Portland to Fryeburg. The Bangor and Aroostook Railroad runs a snow train from Bangor to Greenville on the same day.

Aurele Legere from Rumford wins the Eastern Amatuer Jumping Championship in Brattleboro, Vermont.

The CCC cuts trails on Pleasant Mountain, Mt. Blue, Mt. Megunticook, Mt Desert and Bigelow Mtn.
1935

Nautilus Ski & Pontoon Co. introduces the Trailmaster, one of the first laminated skis. It was guaranteed not to break.

The second and last Bangor to Caribou marathon is held.

Hussey Manufacturing in N. Berwick helps the ski industry by designing lifts, jumps, ski trails and toboggan chutes.

Fort Fairfield holds the Tri-Town Ski Marathon.
1937

World War II puts a stop to skiing's growth. Ski areas in Maine shut down their rope tows for lack of gas to run the engines. Paris Manufacturing and Bass Shoes switch to military products.

Post World War II Skiing grows rapidly as army surplus equipment becomes available. Skiers across Maine open new areas as thousands of people take lessons and become avid skiers.

1926
Birger Olsen proposes a Winter Sports Park at the Expo in Portland.

A grueling 110 mile race from Portland to Berlin, New Hampshire promotes the opening of the Berlin Winter Carnival.

1929
The Great Depression puts a brake on most leisure time and sport. The growth of skiing levels off.

1936
The first 200 mile Bangor to Caribou ski marathon promotes the Caribou Winter Carnival.

Maine's first rope tow opens on Jockey Cap in Fryeburg. A scant two weeks later Maine's second rope tow opens at Bridgton Highlands in Bridgton.

The *Portland Press Herald* begins *"Along the Snow Trail"*, a weekly section of the paper devoted to skiing.

1938
The rope tow is moved from Bridgton Highlands to the bottom of the racing trail on Pleasant Mountain.

A super-modern ski resort is planned on Mt. Waldo, south of Bangor. Airplanes would land on the granite peak and skiers would be brought back to the top by wagons pulled by tractors.

Lost Maine Ski Areas

"ONE OF THE SPORTIEST TRAILS

IN MAINE, A NEWLY CUT COURSE

ON MT. OSSIPEE, IS NOW READY

FOR SKI ENTHUSIASTS."

BALD MOUNTAIN—In the late 1930s the Penobscot Valley Ski Club provided a ski patrol, maintained trails and a shelter on Bald Mountain in Dedham. By 1969 the area had 12 trails, 20 acres of open slope, night skiing and called itself "Maine's Biggest Little Ski Area".

BAUNEG BEG SKI CLUB SLOPE—Beginning in 1936 the Bauneg Beg (pronounced Bonny Beg) Ski Club ran a rope tow on an open slope in North Berwick. As club members improved their skiing they began to look for a bigger hill. They found it a few miles north in Newfield, they picked up the tow and moved.

BEAVER HILL—In the 1930s the open slope on Beaver Hill, Springvale, was used by skiers who climbed to ski. By the late 1960s Nasson College was running a rope tow on the hill. The view of Mount Agamenticus, Bauneg Beg Mt. and east to the waters of the Atlantic Ocean is beautiful.

BELFAST—The sign read simply "Ski Area". "The area was a community project in the late 1960s," says Chris Kinney, a high school student at the time. "The rope tow was built by the Lions Club using poles donated by Central Maine Power and an engine donated by a local machine shop. We skied on three trails, which were really quite steep, and a 15 meter jump. A lot of school ski meets were held at the area. "It was a lot of fun, there was something for everybody. People rode flying saucers down the landing hill of the jump." After six years of operation the area closed in 1973. There had been problems with the engine and with the rope. "The rope was made out of hemp and some kids thought they could smoke it. We kept losing sections," says Kinney.

BELL SKI AREA—A rope tow was available to skiers at this area in Lewiston in the late 1960s.

BETHEL—In the 1930s there were several trails around Bethel. The Devil's Kitchen Trail was an expert trail but the top was flat. A wooden 20' tower gave skiers more speed and made the first turn more exciting. By 1950 there was a 1,000' rope tow, lights and a heated snack bar on the Bethel Ski Slope.

BIJAH HILL SKI AREA—Located in Starks, there was one rope tow during the 1960s.

BLACK CAT—"North of Millinockett are two trails, each about 1/2 mile long. The MOC trail is 12-30 feet wide and the North Trail is 15-30 feet wide. Both have northern exposure. In addition there is a toboggan slide, a small ski jump and a large lodge with cooking equipment for visitors," wrote *Maine For Winter Sports* in 1940.

BLACKSTRAP SLOPE—Open in the 1950s Blackstrap, in Cumberland, offered a 1,000' rope tow with a vertical drop of 200'. Slopes were lighted for night skiing and instruction was available.

BRADBURY MOUNTAIN STATE PARK—The Ski Instructors Association of Maine ran a ski proficiency program for elementary school students at this ski area in Pownal. "The impelling force to make skiing available to all Maine children stems from a sincere moral obligation to encourage clean, healthful recreation," wrote *The Pine Cone* in 1949. The program was so popular it was also run at Lake St. George and Quoggy Jo ski areas.

BRADLEY MOUNTAIN SKI SLOPE— In the late 1940s the Bowdoin Outing Club ran a lean-to shelter and a ski trail on this mountain in Topsham.

■ **BRIDGTON HIGHLANDS**—Ice skating, toboggan chute, narrow gauge train rides and an electric rope tow for skiers were all offered in Bridgton to the winter sports enthusiast. "Several double runner bobsleds have been unearthed around town and beginning this week the snow fans looking for the thrill of a bobsled ride can slide to their hearts content," wrote the *Portland Press Herald* in 1936. In 1938 the tow was moved to Pleasant Mountain where there was a bigger ski hill.

■ **BURNT MEADOW**—Since the devastating forest fires in 1947, Brownfield was one of the most depressed towns in Maine. In 1969 the Farmers Home Administration approved a $425,000 loan to build Burnt Meadow Ski Area and Golf Center. The project doubled the property valuation of Brownfield and was expected to provide 25 jobs. "I bought the area in 1980 mostly for the lifts," says Wendell Pierce, owner of Big Rock Ski Area. "The townspeople really didn't want me to remove the lifts, so my daughter ran the area for a couple of years. The area just wasn't going to make money so I had to close it."

■ **CAMDEN HILLS STATE PARK**—In the Camden Hills the CCC cut a cross country trail, two downhill ski trails and built a large ski shelter with two fireplaces. The Mount Megunticook Trail was hand graded, 30 to 60' wide, over a mile long with a drop of 1,000'. In the 1930s a number of races were held on this trail and it was sometimes called simply the Slalom Trail.

■ **CARIBOU**—"The city provides excellent skiing facilities," wrote *Skiing In The East* in 1939. "Included are three ski trails, an equal number of open slopes and three ski jumps.

The longest ski marathon course in the United States runs from Bangor to Caribou – 180 miles long. Winter horse racing and sled dog races are held here, and the Aroostook River provides an ideal spot for ice fishing. The sports season is brought to a climax with a winter carnival featuring a marathon run over the Caribou to Bangor course."

■ **DEVILS DUMP**—"When we were kids in Gorham in the 1930s we followed the road in from the farm and across the brook," says Walter Soule. The brook cut through layers of soft glacial till to form a deep ravine. "We skied mostly on the west side because it was steeper. It was all open then, oh there were a few alders in the bottom we would run into. My father installed metal edges on the wooden skis for all the kids in the neighborhood. He also made rope tow grippers out of barn door hinges."

■ **DEXTER WINTER SPORTS AREA**—There was a rope tow at this area in Dexter in the 1960s.

■ **DOUGLAS MOUNTAIN**—"Douglas Mountain, in Sebago, provides some of the best open slopes anywhere near Portland, affording learning skiers, of whom there are many in Portland, splendid opportunities to test their newly acquired skills on not-too-steep ski runs," wrote the *Portland Press Herald* in February, 1936.

■ **DUNDEE HEIGHTS**—Before World War II skiers used this open slope in North Gorham. After the war a rope tow and lights were installed. Cross-country trails were also available.

■ **DUNHAMS MT. FARM SKI SLOPE**—"More than 10,000 people gathered for the dedication of Dunham Ski Hill in Waterville, where Governor Barrows headed the official party," wrote the *Portland Press Herald* in January, 1938. Governor Barrows hailed the new winter sports development as "unequaled in Maine" and pledged assistance of the state government in the promotion of this and other winter sports areas. The governor further predicted that with continued development, the Maine winter sports business eventually would equal the tourist industry as a factor in Maine prosperity. Snow trains ran that day from Portland and Bangor. Despite a freezing rain thousands of others arrived by car and walked the last mile, as the road was jammed with cars. The lighted slope offered Maine's longest ski tow, a 1200' rope tow, skiing for novices, intermediates, a slalom hill for experts and a toboggan chute. Overnight facilities and lunches were offered in the ski lodge.

■ ENCHANTED MOUNTAIN—"Enjoy skiing at Enchanted Mountain, a new ski resort designed to excite and challenge skiers of all ages," said the brochure. "A unique new chalet overlooks Moosehead Lake and a panoramic view of vast, rugged mountain ranges. Come to Enchanted Mountain, the 'Switzerland of Maine' where the skiing is fun and exciting." The area opened February, 1966 and closed in the spring of 1974. The last few years locals struggled to keep the area open but the setting in Jackman was too far removed from the skiers.

■ EVERGREEN VALLEY— The 1960s saw a great number of new ski areas open in Maine and the planning board in Stoneham began an ambitious ski area project. After years of planning, building and several changes in ownership Evergreen Valley finally opened in 1973, the year of the energy crisis. The following year was one of the lowest snowfalls on record. Financial and legal problems grew and the area closed in 1975.

■ FRYEBURG—When the snow train arrived from Portland in 1935 beginners rode a horse-drawn hay wagon to Pine Hill for lessons. Others rode to Jockey Cap, the site of Maine's first rope tow. Jockey Cap also had a toboggan chute and later a second, wood sided toboggan chute. Behind the train station were trails on Starks Mountain. Because these trails were steep and narrow they were only for the better skiers. While waiting for the train at the end of the day, novice skiers watched experts ski the S turns at the bottom of Starks Mountain.

■ GREENVILLE— Seeing the excitement over the train from Portland to Fryeburg, officials of the Bangor and Aroostook Railroad made a last minute decision to run a ski train from Bangor to Greenville. The local CCC camp helped the townspeople of Greenville prepare for the train. The trip was a big success and was repeated each year. In February, 1937 the *Bangor Daily News* wrote, "Reports say the snow conditions are ideal and that a ski jump, toboggan slide, skating rink, and ski trail will be available for snow patrons. As usual the Snow Train will be heated during the layover in Greenville and may be used as a headquarters for the passengers." Skiers and tobogganers slid down the hill and across the ice of Shadow Pond.

■ GUILFORD KIWANIS SKI AREA— The Guilford Kiwanis club cleared a slope in the 1960s and ran a 500' rope tow.

■ HI POINT TOW—In the early 1950s this area, which was part of Augusta's municipal recreation program, had a 400' rope tow and skiing on several open slopes.

■ HOBBS HILL—Skiers on the wide, natural, hillside above Crystal Lake in Harrison had a variety of slopes to choose from. A rope tow ran from 1937 until World War II.

■ HOTHAM'S HILL SKI AREA—Located in Auburn, the area had one rope tow in the 1960s.

■ **KINGS MOUNTAIN SLOPE** — In the late 1930s novice skiers used this open slope in Bangor. After the war a 700' rope tow was installed.

■ **LAKE ST. GEORGE STATE PARK**—The area located in Liberty was called Snowflake by the locals. The rope tow was built shortly after World War II and was run by a truck on blocks. The main trail was the Lake View Trail which was wide and 2100' long. A one room lodge with picture windows looked out over the lake. To groom the slope a snowmobile dragged implements. Lights provided night skiing.

Wooden rope tow gripper, 1940s

■ **LINCOLN MUNICIPAL SKI AREA**— A rope tow served this municipal area in Lincoln during the 1960s.

■ **MADAWASKA SKI SLOPE**—Located in Grand Isle just off Route 1, the area had a 2,000' rope tow that serviced an open slope.

■ **MAGGIE'S MOUNTAIN SKI AREA**—"There was no Maggie, it was just a made-up name," says Elaine Polakewich from Freeport. "I wanted to start a business and decided to open a ski area. I didn't ski but wanted to do something. In 1962 I opened the ski area on a small hill with a short rope tow. I had a team of horses and we had sleigh rides and parties. We closed after a few years."

■ **MARS HILL**—The hills of Aroostook County are mostly low, rolling rises. Glaciers ground down the hills and crushed the underlying limestone rock into the fertile soil that makes the County famous for its potatoes. In the middle of this flat topography stands one big rock, Mars Hill, that has been home to three ski

areas. In 1937 a two and a half mile downhill trail was cut from the summit for races in the Mars Hill Winter Carnival. In 1954 a second area opened on the mountain. "Vaugn Cole of Coles Express and Carol Anderson, a local farmer, put a rope tow on the back of what is now Big Rock ski area," says Wendell Pierce, owner of Big Rock, the third area to be on Mars Hill. "They used one of the trucks from Coles Express and ran the rope around the rear wheels. They had quite a little development. It was a nice hill, steep for the times. They ran it for a couple of years but it wasn't the right time."

■ **McFARLAND'S SKI AREA**—In the late 1930s the Mt. Desert Island Outing Club ran a 800' long rope tow and a practice hill. The tow was later lengthened to 1350' and several trails were added. There were ten acres of glade skiing and lights for night skiing. The island has many miles of carriage roads built for horse drawn carriages, those beginning at the foot of McFarland's Hill were used for cross-country skiing. Horses from the stables were used for sleighing and skijoring.

■ **MOUNT GILE SKI AREA**—The East Auburn Community Unit sponsored and ran a rope tow on Mt. Giles in the 1960s. "We ran the area for the community and mostly for the East Auburn kids," says Glen Burgess, one of the members. "Kids from East Auburn skied for free, everybody else had to pay $1. Weekends were busy and vacation week in February was the best. Everybody had a good time."

■ **MOUNT QUITO**—Open for three years (from 1939 to 1941), a rope tow, lodge and several trails were available at this area in Casco. High school skiers stopped skiing there when the owner refused to let a Jewish friend ski.

■ **MUNICIPAL SKI SLOPE**—A short ski from Millinockett, this 1/4 mile trail was hand graded in the late 1930s to provide early season skiing. After the war a rope tow, ski hut, lunch bar and lights were added.

■ **NOPAR SKI AREA**—"In 1947 my brother, Lester, my wife, Jeannette and I bought a rope tow and set it up on Pike's Hill," says Albert Soule from South Paris. "We called it the Norway-South Paris Ski Area and shortened it to Nopar. We discovered you can't run a ski area and do much skiing so we sold the tow. We didn't get much money for it but at least we could ski again."

■ **NORTH'S HILL SKI SLOPE**—The Wilton Community Ski Tow Association ran a 400' rope tow and extensive children's programs in the 1950s.

■ **OPPORTUNITY FARM FOR BOYS**— In the 1940s this private school in New Gloucester used a tractor to provide power for a rope tow for students.

■ **OSSIPEE MOUNTAIN**—"One of the sportiest trails in Maine, a newly cut course on Mt. Ossipee in Waterboro, is now ready for ski enthusiasts," wrote *Along The Snow Trail* in January, 1936. "The trail was plotted and cut by the Hock-amock Ski Club, an organization largely composed of Portland skiers. The trail is one mile long and winds down over the steep sides of Mt. Ossipee, providing fast curves that will tax the skill of the most experienced skiers. A farmhouse near the summit has been reno-vated as a headquarters for the club."

■ **OXFORD HILLS**—"Plans for an elaborate lay-out of ski trails in the Oxford Hills are being formulated by the Skovstiers Ski Club of Lewiston," wrote *Along The Snow Trail* in

February, 1936. "Trails of all degrees of difficulty are proposed for Little Singepole Mt. and Streaked Mt. Harry Davis, secretary of the Skovstiers, said, 'Opening of this section of the Oxford Hills to skiing is an important forward step in the growth of skiing interest'."

■ **PARADISE PARK**—The site of the Bangor Winter carnival ski events, the park was open from 4:00 each afternoon until midnight. "The rope tow is the only one of its kind in Eastern Maine at the present," wrote the *Bangor Daily News* in February, 1937. "Such a mechanical gadget has become exceedingly popular with winter sports fans offering a ride back up steep hills, enabling skiers to enjoy themselves to a greater extent."

■ **PINE HAVEN SKI AREA** —In the 1960s skiers in Lewiston used the rope tow at this area.

■ **POLAND SPRING**—Hiram Ricker kept his famous resort open for winter visitors in 1916. Lessons were offered in both cross-country and jumping. Due to the expense of heating the resort they stopped staying open winters in the late 1920s. In the 1960s the Job Corps built a 2,000' T-bar serving two trails, an open slope and a cross-country trail. Expenses outweighed income and the area closed again.

■ **POPLAR RIDGE**—The slope in Falmouth was fairly flat and was for beginners who were not able to handle the steeper slopes at nearby Hurricane Mountain.

■ **QUODDY SKI CLUB DEVELOPMENT**—After World War II, skiers downeast in Pembroke used a rope tow built on an open slope.

■ **ROTARY PARK**—Municipal ski slopes, such as this one in Biddeford from the 1960s, introduced skiing to many people. After years of sitting idle, the rope tow was sold to Richard Legere who is currently using it at Bauneg Beg Ski Trails.

■ **SABATTUS MOUNTAIN**—The Skovstiers Trail was cut on Sabattus Mt. east of Lewiston in late 1935. The trail was 12-30' wide, 1/3 mile long, had a drop of 600' and was rated expert. The Skovstiers Ski Club planned and cut this trail along with others in the Oxford Hills.

■ **SHERIDAN MOUNTAIN**— Sam Ouellette, who gained fame as a ski marathoner, designed and ran a ski center in Ashland after World War II. A rope tow, practice slopes and trails for both downhill and, of course, cross-country skiing were available. "A few years ago I bought the mountain," says Wendell Pierce the owner of Big Rock Ski Area. "Sam Oullette's area had been closed for a while. I had a bulldozer go up and put in some trails then I got more involved with Big Rock so I backed out of putting in the rope tow there. We had set the poles, put in the trails and put in the septic system. I never got my project off the ground."

■ **SHOREACRES SKI SLOPE**—"The ski slope in Bowdoinham was popular before the war but has been used little during the past few years," wrote the *Brunswick Record* in January, 1947. "Constance Luce bought the property in 1946," says Billy Oakes, the current owner. "She put a hardwood floor in the big barn for dances. The orchestra played in the hayloft. The smaller barn was used as a snack bar and warming hut. She built a 600' rope tow. You could ski or ride a toboggan down the hill, onto a spit of land and then onto the frozen ice of Merrymeeting Bay. The National Ski Patrol and the

Professional Ski Instructors Association Of Maine provided their services. Mrs. Luce ran the area until she sold the property in 1955."

■ **SILVER HILLS SKI AREA**— Three rope tows ran on weekends at this area in Augusta. In the 1960s the area offered free ski school clinics and specialized in family skiing.

■ **SKI HAVEN**— In the 1930s the Deering High School Ski Club used a cottage on Dyke Mountain in Sebago as their ski center. Students cut seven trails, built bunks, installed a wood stove and decorated the cottage with ski posters and framed pictures of skiers in action. After Mrs. Dyke passed away, a group of Deering skiers and their parents bought the Dyke Farm. During World War II this was a popular place for Deering skiers to go. "It wasn't easy to get around during the war," says Sarah Cowan. "There wasn't much money and because of rationing there wasn't much gas. We took the train from Portland to West Baldwin, then we would hike six miles in to Dyke Mountain. We always had fun."

■ **SKI-HORSE MOUNTAIN SKI AREA**—Located in Newburgh during the 1960s, there was both a rope tow and a T-bar.

■ **SKY HY PARK**—In 1939 two trails and two open slopes were skied. Plans for a lodge and several ski jumps at this site in Topsham never materialized due to World War II. In 1962 Sky-Hy ski area opened on the same hill and offered ten trails serviced by a T-bar. Trails, with names such as Big Dipper and Little Dipper, were all named after constellations.

■ **SNOW FLAKE SKI AREA**—Loring Air Force Base in Limestone ran a small area with a T-bar until the base shut down in 1992.

SNOW MOUNTAIN SKI AREA— Located in Winterport, the area opened in the 1960s with a T-bar, rope tow, two slopes, seven trails, ski school and rentals.

SOLDIER POND SKI AREA—"For a thrill-Ride in our Aerial Tramway, whether skiing or not," said the ad for Soldier Pond Ski Area in Soldier Pond. Walter Stadig's "Aerial Tramway" was Maine's first chair when he installed it in 1946. Stadig's lift kept the skier low to the ground; skis stayed in contact with the snow. To increase uphill capacity Stadig tied a rope to the chair. One person sat on the chair and the other grabbed the rope and was towed up the hill.

SPRING HILL SKI AREA—Opened in the early 1960s with a Penny Pitou Ski School, this area in South Berwick was an excellent learning hill. Skiers on the small hill, about 80' tall, skied down to the pond and rode a rope tow back up. Toboggans also slid out onto the ice. Horses were used to haul the toboggans back up the hill. Skiing lasted only for a few years before a couple of bad snow winters, and an exodus of skiers to bigger hills, forced the tow to close.

STREAKED MOUNTAIN SKI CLUB—When you look at the mountain from South Paris you see a wide streak of rock coming from the summit most of the way down. In 1940, *Maine For Winter Sports* wrote, "The old Mountain Schoolhouse is being used as a clubhouse. A very fast trail suitable for experts is being developed right from the top of the mountain over the ledges and down through the wooded area." "It was beautiful, open skiing if you hit it just right but those ledges don't hold the snow," says Albert Soule from South Paris. "The wind blew snow off and the sun melted the rest."

Maine made Bass boot from the 1940s

STROUDWATER—Skiers used the fields by the Stroudwater River in Portland instead of taking the snow train to Fryeburg or the buses to Ossipee Mountain. "On Saturday afternoons Max Weildon will impart the latest wrinkles in ski technique on the slopes at Stroudwater," wrote the *Portland Press Herald* in February, 1936. "Taking full advantage of unusually fast running conditions for so early in the season the Deering High School Ski Club put in busy sessions daily on their practice slopes at Stroudwater in preparation for a meet there on Saturday." In 1936 there was even talk about installing lights for night skiing.

VEAZIE SKI AREA—Located in Veazie, this area had a rope tow during the 1960s.

WESTERN MOUNTAIN—"The new ski course on Western Mountain in Southwest Harbor is extremely scenic, providing widespread coastal and mountain views," wrote *Along The Snow Trail* in February, 1937. "Completed last week by the CCC the trail will provide a speedy downhill run. A maximum speed of 60 miles an hour is believed possible on the trail which has some straight 'shusses' over slopes with a drop of 40 to 50 degrees."

WESTERN VIEW SLOPE—A rope tow was built on the Western View Golf Club in Augusta in the 1960s.

WITS-END SKI SLOPE— Located on the Johnson Farm in Wiscasset, Wits-End Ski Slope had a 650' rope tow and lights for night skiing.

Current Maine Ski Areas

WE JACKED UP A TRACTOR, CUT

GROOVES IN THE REAR TIRE AND RAN

THE ROPE AROUND THAT. THE TOW

WAS JUST FOR OURSELVES, BUT THE

FIRST THING WE KNEW THERE WERE

PEOPLE COMING FROM EVERYWHERE,

CARS LINED THE STREET.

BAKER MOUNTAIN—In the late 1930s Allen Quimby Jr. operated a veneer mill in Bingham. Quimby liked to ski so he built a 1200' rope tow on nearby Mt. Baker. By 1940 a second tow had been added; one served an open slope, the other brought skiers to the Baker Mountain Trail. Later, another tow brought skiers from the top of the open slope to the top of the mountain. In 1969 the rope tows were replaced with a T-bar. Surrounding towns contribute money to operate the area. Season pass holders or club members volunteer to maintain and run the area. During February vacation week they offer a School on Skis, free ski lessons, to anyone who wants to learn how to ski. Towns loan school buses to bring kids skiing during vacation week.

■ **BAUNEG BEG SKI TRAILS**—"My wife and I drove around the countryside looking for a good hill with a For Sale sign on it," says Richard Legere. "We found the right hill on Bauneg Beg Mountain in Berwick. We built our house ten years ago and have been skiing here since 1990." Legere bought the tow from the city of Biddeford where it had been used at Rotary Park. He rebuilt the tow and operates it for himself and friends. The hill has 110' vertical serviced by the 340' long tow. I set up a snowmaking system so we can start the season with a good base. In 1994 we skied until April 1. I don't charge people to ski here because then I would need insurance and I can't afford it. I do this because I love to ski. Last year we operated for 79 days and a few moonlit nights."

■ **BIG ROCK**—Alaska and Hawaii had just become the 49th and 50th states and the people of Mars Hill wanted to celebrate. The Junior Chamber of Commerce decided to start a ski area on Mars Hill and to raise a flag at the top on July 4th. "We used all kinds of different projects to raise money," says Wendell Pierce, the current owner. "One time we blocked off U.S. Route 1, put up a toll gate and collected money from everyone who came through. The state police were right there cheering us on. Another time we had a Jailbird Jamboree. We 'arrested' people and they had to get bailed out. We arrested the state police and all the local VIPs. When the bus came through we arrested the driver and all the passengers chipped in to get him back so they could get home. Our first lift was a Poma lift. When it arrived in New York City it took us another month to get money to ship it here. It took us most of the winter to get the lift installed and we finally got it going in March, 1961. Interest was so great, we have almost never had more people skiing than we did those first three weekends."

■ **BLACK MOUNTAIN**—"In the 1920s most of the skiing in Rumford was done at the Spruce Street Area which was walking distance from town," says Aurele Legere, the 1936 Eastern Ski Jumping Champion. "We jumped at Spruce Street until the jump keeled over in 1942. After the war we jumped at Scotty's Mountain. We kept enlarging that jump and the record on that hill was 202'. When the owner of Scotty's Mountain died in the 1950s there were too many heirs so we looked around and developed Black Mountain. In the 1950s the Chisolm Ski Club bought the land on Black Mountain. There was very little downhill skiing around Rumford, we mostly jumped, but then someone had to invent a rope tow to drag up those alpine skiers. We built a real nice jump there.

Think Snow!

WORLD WAR II FOUND RUSS HAGGETT WORKING AS A BOSS SHIPFITTER IN THE SHIP YARDS OF SOUTH PORTLAND AND THEN AS A SEABEE IN THE PACIFIC. HE PUT TOGETHER A PARTNERSHIP THAT BOUGHT LAND FOR THE SKI AREA. WHEN RUSS RETURNED TO BRIDGTON IN 1946 HE BECAME MANAGER OF PLEASANT MOUNTAIN SKI AREA. HE CUT NEW TRAILS AND ENLARGED THE BASE LODGE. IN 1951 HE REPLACED ONE OF THE ROPE TOWS WITH MAINE'S FIRST T-BAR. IN 1954 HE BUILT A CHAIR LIFT TO THE TOP OF THE MOUNTAIN. FOR MANY YEARS THIS WAS THE ONLY CHAIR LIFT IN THE STATE.

RUSS SET HIGH STANDARDS FOR HIS SKI AREA. THE KITCHEN ALWAYS HAD MODERN APPLIANCES AND GOOD FOOD. SOME PEOPLE WENT TO THE MOUNTAIN JUST FOR A CUP OF COFFEE AND A FRESH RAISED DONUT. RUSS OFFERED FREE SKIING AND LESSONS TO THE BRIDGTON KIDS ON THURSDAY AFTERNOONS. IN PART HE WANTED TO SHARE HIS LOVE OF SKIING WITH THE KIDS AND IN PART IT WAS A SHREWD BUSINESS MOVE, AS MANY OF THOSE KIDS ENDED UP BUYING SEASON PASSES.

"RUSS HAD A BUMPER STICKER THAT SAID 'THINK SNOW!....RUSS HAGGETT'," REMEMBERS MIKE RICHARDS, ONE OF THOSE KIDS WHO WAS HOOKED ON SKIING BY THE FREE THURSDAYS. "KNOWING RUSS WE KNEW THIS WAS NOT A SUGGESTION BUT RATHER A COMMAND."

"ILLNESS FORCED RUSS TO TAKE A LESS DEMANDING JOB," SAID HIS SISTER ROWENA. "HE DROVE BY THE MOUNTAIN ON WEEKENDS TO SEE THE LARGE CROWDS THAT WERE SKIING AND HE SILENTLY WISHED THEM GOOD LUCK WITH HIS BELOVED MOUNTAIN."

More people started to ski downhill, so we also cut some ski trails and put in a lift for them."

■ **BREAKNECK MOUNTAIN**—"My father used to run Sunrise Ski Area on this mountain in Alexander, east of Machias" says Jim Davis. Last year we skied on one trail, I have five others roughed out. The trail is 30' wide, maybe a little less where it is steep, it's hard to lug a chainsaw on the steep slope. I hope to get a lift but now we use a snowmobile to get up the mountain. The problem is finding someone to drive the snowmobile back down. Other areas argue about who has the fastest lift in the east or most snowmaking in the east, but I have the eastest area in the east."

■ **CAMDEN SNOW BOWL** -"By August, 1936 the Camden Outing Club formed plans for the proposed winter sports area at Hosmer's Pond," wrote Jack Williams in The *History of Camden*. "Plans called for ski trails, a rope tow, several toboggan chutes, ski jumps, as well as a lodge house. On the pond, it was planned to have a hockey rink, a track for horse racing, a skating area and room for ice boating. There was a tremendous amount of town spirit for this project!" That fall a raft was made from telephone poles to ferry material across the pond for the lodge. Twenty tons of granite blocks were ferried across for the two fireplaces. "Some 1,000 people had been involved in the project as volunteers or donors of food and money," wrote Williams. "Open house for the new facility was held on the weekend of January 15 & 16, 1937 with hundreds in attendance. A light snowfall permitted use of the toboggan chute for the first time. "With the help of volunteers and the WPA, the ski area was completed. The ski tow went into operation for the first time on January 15, 1939, and skiing became a favorite sport in the area."

EATON MOUNTAIN — Carlton Bosworth was an early recreational skier who skied on Eaton Mountain in Skowhegan in the late 1920s. By the late 1930s there were two trails on the mountain. The war ended skiing on Eaton Mountain. Carlton's son, Ron Bosworth skied at Sugarloaf with his friend Paul Sylvain in the late 1950s. Paul did construction work and had little work or income during the winter. He saw a way to ski frequently and to generate more income for his family. "Why not make our own ski area?" Paul asked his father, Paul Sr. and brother, Larry. Together the Sylvains bought the land, cut three trails, built a rope tow, a lodge and opened for the winter of 1961-62.

HERMON MOUNTAIN SKI AREA — "My son, Bernard, learned to ski in high school," says Barbara Jackson. "Albert, my husband, was doing some logging on the hill behind our house. Bernard and his chums climbed the tote roads and skied down. Albert started cutting his tote roads so they would be better to ski on. In the late 1960s we decided to open the trails to the public. We installed a rope tow and a few years later a T-bar, snowmaking and lights. Running a ski area is a challenge but we liked to be outdoors and we liked to work hard. We lost the area a few years ago, before Albert died. I still cross-country ski and can hear the kids hollering and having fun as they ski. It is very gratifying."

KENTS HILL SKI SLOPE — Bill Dunn wanted Kents Hill School, a private high school in Kents Hill, to offer skiing to its students. In 1942 he hired "Pug" Goldthwait from Dartmouth to find the appropriate hill, clear the terrain and start a ski program, one of the first coed high school ski programs in the nation. A rope tow was installed in the early 1950s, lights, snowmaking and a groomer in the mid 1980s. Today nearly half the student body is involved in skiing and both the men's and women's teams won the New England Prep School Championships in 1995.

LONESOME PINES — The area opened in 1968 at the end of Route 1 in Fort Kent. "They looked at a bigger mountain about five miles out of town," says Mike Voisine the area manager. "The decision was to build the ski area in town so the kids can walk to it. The area is open for skiing on Wednesday and Friday nights. We have a rope tow for the beginners and a T-bar. From the beginning the area has been membership owned; if you buy a season pass you get a say in the running of the area."

LOST VALLEY — "I owned an apple orchard in Auburn and wanted to offer my key employees year round work," says Otto Wallingford. "I had done some skiing and we had a good hill, so in September, 1960 we broke ground and in January we opened Lost Valley Ski Area. We drove one of the farm tractors to the top and ran the rope tow off that. Two weeks after we opened there was an ice storm. I had read an article in *Readers Digest* about snowmaking and so we bought a snow gun from Larchmont. We had snowmaking going about two weeks after that ice storm. I invented the powder maker that was pulled behind a snow cat to break up the hard snow. We tried everything to loosen the snow. They all left the snow lumpy. Then the idea of the powder maker came to me. We built one and after 30' I knew it was going to work. We always stressed the importance of our ski school. A few years after we opened we were doing 3,200 lessons a week. We taught a lot of people to ski and I think that is the biggest contribution we made to skiing."

■ MAY MOUNTAIN—

The area in Island Falls opened in the late 1960s by two doctors who loved to ski. By the late 1980s it was run down and neglected. The owners tried to sell the T-bar and close the area. Locals pulled together and bought the ski area in 1992. Today it is run by local investors basically for themselves and their kids. "Parents feel very comfortable leaving their kids at the area and knowing that they will be watched over," says general manager Christie Branson. Surrounding terrain is fairly steep and there are a number of lakes.

■ MOUNT ABRAMS—

Three brothers, Stuart, Donald and Norton Cross owned a family woodlot on Mt. Abram in Locke Mills. One day while Norton was working near the top of the mountain he looked down into the valley and realized what a good ski mountain the brothers had. "It looked to us as though other people were making millions with ski lodges," said Norton. "We've found out it's not that simple." When the area opened in 1960 the grooming equipment consisted of the three brothers climbing up and down the mountain wearing snowshoes. Before today's hightech grooming machines and aggressive snowmaking Don became an expert at cutting trails with bays for the wind to drift snow into, thus using the mountain and nature to its best advantage. "Years ago, we made our skis ourselves out of white pine and used an old inner tube for a binding," Stuart said in an interview with *Downeast* magazine in 1977.

"Now that we have a ski area we don't have much time for skiing."

■ MOUNT JEFFERSON—

"We weren't skiers but we wanted to try it," says Byron Delano. "We read about Sugarloaf and visited it. In 1963 six of us built a rope tow on a back road a couple of miles from here. We jacked up a tractor, cut grooves in the rear tire and ran the rope around that. The tow was just for ourselves, but the first thing we knew there were people coming from everywhere, cars lined the street. We got a truck with a hot dog stand on the back and started selling hot dogs. That got us going and we decided to open a ski area. Looking around we found Mt. Jefferson right here in Lee. A local woodsman agreed to cut three trails for the wood on them. We spent $20,000 and had a T-bar installed for the winter of 1964. In 1980 I bought out my five partners. I was a potato farmer and didn't have much to do in the winter so this gave us something to do. Now it seems like a year round job preparing the trails and everything else."

■ PINNACLE SKI CLUB—

A Kiwanis project in Pittsfield, the area opened in the late 1950s with a rope tow. A few years later the Pinnacle Ski Club split off from Kiwanis and took over the operation of the area. A second rope tow was built on the bunny hill, with a smaller diameter rope so kids with their smaller hands could hold the rope. "Parents who learned to ski at the area are now bringing their kids to learn," says Don Woodruff, a club member. "In some cases we are on our third generation. A family membership is $35. You get lessons on Saturday mornings and skiing but you also must pledge time to help in the kitchen or on the hill."

■ **POWDER HOUSE HILL SKI AREA**—In the 1930s skiers climbed Powder House Hill in South Berwick to ski. After World War II the Agamenticus Ski Club drove a 1938 Ford truck to the top and used it to power a rope tow. In 1950, when the area was not a commercial success, the Powder House Ski Club was formed to run the area. "That 1938 truck was difficult to find parts for and to repair," says Bob Lane, one of the club members. "We mounted a new air cooled engine on the back and ran the tow with that." A building now encloses the engine, but the rusting cab sticks out the back. "The idea was to have local skiing," says Bruce Martin, a current club member. "A lot of people left Powder House Ski Club when Big A opened. About ten years later, in 1979, Big A had closed and we reopened Powder House Ski Area. Families get involved because they have kids. It's convenient in terms of cost and driving to teach your kids locally. Powder House Ski Area brings people together. It's fun."

■ **QUOGGY JO SKI CENTER**—Depending heavily on volunteer labor and donations the Quoggy Jo Ski Club moved their tow from Stevens Hill, where it had been for one year, to a hill outside Presque Isle in 1959. Volunteers cleared the slope, set the poles for the tow, bulldozed the tow line and built a hut. Club president Dick Holmes described what happened next in a newsletter to members, "Where are the skiers? Where the hell is the rope? It finally arrived in a December blizzard, 10 degrees below. Now the long buildup pays, the rope is hauled around and spliced (in the back seat of a car). It worked!! And lo - skiers appeared through swirling snow."

Ski All Day Dance All Night

"AMOS COULD SKI ALL DAY AND DANCE ALL NIGHT," RECALLS STUB TAYLOR, SKI PATROL DIRECTOR AT SUGARLOAF. "IN THE 1930S HE TOOK US SKIING AT TUCKERMANS. ON THE WAY BACK AMOS ALWAYS LIKED TO STOP AT THE TOP HAT, BETWEEN BETHEL AND RUMFORD, TO DANCE FOR A FEW HOURS. SOMETIMES WE'D JUST SLEEP IN THE TRUCK WAITING FOR HIM."

"DANCING IS THE WAY YOU LIVE," SAID AMOS IN THE EARLY 1960S WHEN HE WAS IN HIS 60S. "IF A NEW DANCE COMES ALONG AND YOU THINK, WELL, THAT'S A FOOL'S DANCE, AND YOU DON'T DO IT, IN A LITTLE WHILE YOU AREN'T THERE AT ALL. LORD, IF YOU JUST SQUARE DANCE AROUND THIS NECK OF THE WOODS YOU WON'T GET ANYWHERE."

AMOS WAS THE FIRST GENERAL MANAGER OF THE NEW SUGARLOAF SKI AREA. HE RAN IT WITH YANKEE THRIFTINESS. ONCE, BEFORE SUGARLOAF OPENED, A PROSPECTIVE INVESTOR WANTED TO SEE THE MOUNTAIN. AMOS SET HIM UP WITH SKIS, BOOTS AND CLIMBING SKINS, THEN CHARGED HIM 50¢ RENTAL FEE. AMOS EVEN MADE MEMBERS OF THE BOARD OF DIRECTORS PAY FOR THEIR SKI TICKETS.

FOR YEARS AMOS DIDN'T INSTALL INDOOR PLUMBING IN THE BASE LODGE. IN THE 1950S WHEN ASKED WHAT IMPROVEMENTS WERE MADE TO HIS AREA HE PROUDLY SAID, "WE JUST INSTALLED THE FINEST TWO-HOLER IN THE STATE OF MAINE".

■ **SADDLEBACK**—"Rangeley decided that it wants to be a year-round vacation sports center," wrote the *Portland Sunday Telegram* in October, 1958. "The town has gone all out to make its dream come true - to build one of the east's finest ski developments, the 'million dollar' Saddleback Mountain project, as it's already known. 'The other night,' Dr. Paul Fichtner, treasurer of the Rangeley-Saddleback Corp. said, 'a boy of 11 came to the door. In his hand was a cloth bag containing $10 in small change he had earned. He wanted to buy a share of stock. Some of the fellows want stock in the worst way. We've let them - young fellows as well as older men - go right out on the mountain and earn their shares by shovel and ax.'" With design help from Sel Hannah, construction began and the area opened for the 1960-61 ski season with a ski lodge made with Maine cedar, an open slope, four trails and two T-bars.

■ **SHAWNEE PEAK**—In the mid 1930s Walter Soule from Portland was driving to North Conway to ski and saw a snow-covered hillside in Bridgton that looked like fun skiing. With the owner's permission, Walter and his ski buddies took down a fence that ran across the hill and skied. Their skiing attracted Russ Haggett and others to the skiing potential of the mountain. The CCC camp based in Bridgton cut two trails from the top. Racing Trail, also known as the Jack Spratt Trail, was one of the best expert trails around. Most of the CCC workers never skied and couldn't imagine how the steep turns at the top could be negotiated. They took tree trunks from the cleared trail and made big banked turns to help the skiers. "Those turns were fun," says Soule, "but they were about six feet tall and every now and then

someone would ski off the top and drop into the woods." In 1938 the rope tow was moved from Pleasant Highlands to the open slope on Pleasant Mountain. The 1940-41 ski guide *Maine For Winter Sports* said that in addition to three trails, "two tows, ice skating, ice fishing, curling, a tobboggan chute with an electric tow-back, a ski hut and every other form of winter sports are available."

■ **SPRUCE MOUNTAIN SKI SLOPE**—On land leased for $1 a year the Spruce Mountain Ski Club opened its rope tow in the early 1960s. Racing became an important part of Spruce almost immediately. An organized race program has been training prospective racers from the second grade and older. When the land was put up for sale in 1988 Jay, Livermore and Livermore Falls bought the land to ensure the continued operation of the area. The area is run by the ski club, and a board from the towns oversees it. From the beginning the club had a close relationship with the paper mills in town who supplied equipment, time and expertise. Lights for night skiing and power and engineering expertise for snowmaking have been provided by the mills.

■ **SQUAW MOUNTAIN**—Legendary trail designer Sel Hannah was a man who knew mountains and skiing; he designed over 300 ski areas in North America. When asked which was his favorite trail, out of the thousands he had designed, he said, "The Penobscot at

A mechanical plastic toy from the 1940s

Squaw Mountain in Greenville. The views from the top of the trail are just wonderful. Once you start skiing down, the trail moves with the terrain of the mountain better than any other I've seen. There is a variety of sharp turns and wide round turns, the pattern is constantly changing. Rolls in the trail are a challenge if you ski them fast, yet by sweeping around them the novice can ski comfortably. The Penobscot is a fun trail for skiers of all abilities."

■ **SUGARLOAF**—"Horace Chapman, Wes Marco and Fletcher Brown, with some help from the state, formed the Maine Ski Council," says Bunny Bass who was running G.H. Bass, the top ski boot maker in the country. "People from all over the state who were involved in skiing met at the Elm House in Auburn. I was asked to be the first President. Our first job was the area development committee. We wanted to find a mountain and build a big ski area to promote skiing in Maine. We looked at Mt. Blue, the Mahoosics, Grafton Notch and Old Speck but nothing that was quite right. I talked with Amos Winter about our search, his reaction was 'What the heck are you guys looking for? If you really want the best mountain we have it right here at Sugarloaf in Carrabassett Valley'." Sel Hannah came over from Franconia to help Amos design the trail. "Amos cut the road in from Rt. 27 and a ski trail to the snowfields from there," says Stub Taylor. "Every weekend in the summer people showed up to help Amos work on the trail. It was hard work so we didn't make it any wider than we had to. The first trail was named Winter's Way after Amos."

■ **SUNDAY RIVER**—The goal of the Bethel Area Development Corporation was to promote tourism and business and, since Bethel was already a popular summer resort, they decided to use skiing as the vehicle. "We knew enough to know that we needed help," says Mike Thurston, one of the members of the Development Corp. "We hired Sel Hannah for $50, which seemed exorbitant, to spend a day with us looking at the mountain. Paul Kailey, coach of the Gould Academy ski team, liked the area where White Heat is now. Sel said it was too steep and moved down the ridge a bit. We scraped together another $50 for Sel to help us lay out the trails. Sunday River Skiway opened December, 1959 with a T-bar that went 2/3 of the way up the mountain." Did the original plan of the Bethel Area Development Corp. work? "We may have started slow, but have you been here recently?" asks Thurston.

■ **TITCOMBS**—The Franklin County Ski and Outing Club in Farmington decided they were ready to build a rope tow. Previous season skiers climbed and, when they could, talked a local farmer into using his horse drawn wagon to bring them to the top. A used rope tow powered by a Model T Ford, lots of volunteer labor and an early snow storm enabled them to open in November, 1940. Lack of manpower and gas rationing forced the area to close during World War II, as did most areas. In 1956 *Downeast Magazine* wrote, "The physical layout of Titcombs operations is impressive enough, but the Club's greatest achievement is the almost professional system in developing young skiers into topflight competitors." Many of those young skiers went on to compete successfully at the national level.

About The Author

GLENN PARKINSON GREW UP IN VERMONT AND FIRST SKIED IN HIS BACK YARD ON WOODEN SKIS WITH LEATHER TOE LOOPS FOR BINDINGS. BIGGER HILLS AND BETTER EQUIPMENT LED TO A LIFELONG PASSION FOR SKIING. INTEREST IN THE PAST AND RESPECT FOR THOSE WHO CREATED SKIING LED TO A COLLECTION OF SKI EQUIPMENT AND BOOKS.

IN 1989 GLENN AND HIS MOTHER EARLINE MARSH STARTED A NEWSLETTER FOCUSED ON THE HISTORY OF SKIING. JOINING WITH THE NEW INTERNATIONAL SKIING HISTORY ASSOCIATION IN 1991 THE NEWSLETTER, *SKIING HERITAGE*, GREW. GLENN EDITED *SKIING HERITAGE* UNTIL EARLY 1994 WHEN HE RESIGNED TO HAVE MORE TIME TO RESEARCH NEW ENGLAND'S SKI HISTORY.

"MUCH OF SKIINGS HISTORY AND HERITAGE HAS NEVER BEEN RECORDED," SAYS GLENN. "EACH YEAR WE LOSE AN IMPORTANT PART OF OUR SPORT. WRITING *FIRST TRACKS* ENABLED ME TO PRESERVE SOME OF MAINE'S SKIING HERITAGE."

FOR THE LAST 14 YEARS GLENN HAS BEEN A FINANCIAL CONSULTANT FOR SMITH BARNEY, AND ITS PREDECESSOR FIRMS, IN PORTLAND MAINE. HE IS CURRENTLY ON THE BOARD OF DIRECTORS OF THE NEW ENGLAND SKI MUSEUM AND OF I.S.H.A. AND ON THE EDITORIAL ADVISORY BOARD OF *SKIING HERITAGE*.

HIS COLLECTION HAS GROWN TO FILL A BARN WITH LIFTS AND EQUIPMENT, AN ATTIC WITH CLOTHING AND MORE EQUIPMENT AND AN OFFICE WITH PHOTOS, MAGAZINES, BROCHURES AND BOOKS.

HE STILL HAS THOSE SKIS FROM WHEN HE WAS THREE.

Really Lost Maine Ski Areas

We have all been skiing along, looking good, when all of a sudden we find ourself on our back sliding down the hill. "What happened?" we asked. We know the answer – snow snakes.

When we got *First Tracks* back from the printer we proudly looked at it then realized areas were missing from the Lost Ski Areas chapter. "What happened?", we asked. But we knew – snow snakes.

So here are Maine's newly found, Lost Ski Areas:

BALD MOUNTAIN—With a great deal of excitement the Bald Mountain Ski Area in Oquossoc opened in 1958. In 1961 the local paper wrote, "The ski area is living up to its purpose to provide entertainment and recreation for the entire family with its addition of a HiFi system. Much to the delight of teenagers, who have made the area a regular after school stop, the outside speakers broadcast music on the slopes. Whether the enthusiasm will last as they find out that all is not rock and roll on the mountain remains to be seen, as records have been selected that will appeal to all ages."

BIG A—Officially it was the Mount Agamenticus Recreation and Ski Area but everyone called it the Big A. Located in the coastal community of York, the area offered spectacular views of the Atlantic Ocean. When it opened in the late 1960s, with night skiing and a chairlift, Big A was one of the major areas in the state. Sea breezes loaded with salt melted snow almost as fast as the snow guns pumped it out and the area was forced to close.

BIGELOW MOUNTAIN—In the 1930s the CCC cut a trail and built a lodge on Bigelow. On Friday nights Amos Winter closed his Kingfield grocery store store at 9:00. Several local kids waited for him and loaded gear into the store's delivery truck. They drove as close to the CCC lodge as they could. "We ended up skiing the last few miles," says Stub Taylor, one of the kids. "We stayed in the lodge Friday and Saturday nights and skied the CCC trails." The creation of Flagstaff Lake blocked the way to the lodge. Amos, Stub and the other skiers looked at Sugarloaf and decided to ski there.

COLBY COLLEGE SKI AREA—Open in Waterville in the 1960s there was a 1200' T-bar serving the intermediate slope, a rope tow for the novice slope and a 32 meter jump.

CONEN SKI DEVELOPMENT—Before World War II there was a ski slope with a 650' rope tow, heated cabin and cross-country trails one mile from South Paris.

DEER HILL—A few miles from Harrison was an open slope with a 1200' rope tow. Skiers climbed another 700' if they wanted to ski the entire slope. "A ski hut with lunch bar, parking, sleighing, tobogganing and ice fishing are available," wrote *Maine for Winter Vacations* in 1950.

GORHAM KIWANIS SKI SLOPE—In 1961 the Gorham Kiwanis Club opened a rope tow on a small hill with lights in the village. The area was run by students from the University of Maine at Portland-Gorham. A ski school, also run by students, offered lessons.

HURRICANE MOUNTAIN—The rope tow opened in 1947 and lights for night skiing were installed a few years later. Expert skiers appreciated this steep hill located in Falmouth. The area closed in the early 1970s due in part to increased insurance costs.

LONE MOUNTAIN—In the late 1930s skiers in Andover had seven ski trails, a ski jump and an open slope to choose from. Trails then were not the wide boulevards we ski today. Bloods Run Trail dropped 2,000' from the top of the mountain and was only 10-15' wide.

■ **PELLETIER HILL**—The Pelletier family ran a rope tow in Fort Kent. "The skiing was demanding because of the steepness of that hill," says Ron Michaud from Van Buren.

■ **PRESTILE'S**—"I grew up [in the 1960s] just outside Caribou," says Ted Gagnon. "I skied across the frozen Aroostook River to ski and ride the T-bar at Prestile's. That T-bar broke down a lot so we ended up climbing. Sometimes when the lift broke down they tied a rope to the back of a ski-do and towed us up."

■ **PUMPKIN RIDGE**—"I liked to ski and wanted my kids to be able to ski," says Lowell Nallar "When Bald Mt. replaced the rope tow in the 1950s a few of us got together, bought it, and put it on Pumpkin Ridge near Machias. The tow took us about 750' up the hill, we climbed up from there. We put up lights and skied at night. We had fun and got a lot of people skiing."

■ **QUOGGY JO**—The ski area on Quoggy Jo Mountain, just south of Presque Isle, was also called Aroostook State Park. An old auto engine was used to pull a large wooden sled, on which the skiers sat, 600' up the hill. The trail was about 2600' long, steep and rocky near the top. It took about three feet of snow to cover all the rocks and open the entire trail. A 600' toboggan chute and a 20 meter ski jump were also available. World War II ended skiing at Quoggy Jo.

■ **RANGELEY**—"We spent an entire fall cutting a ski trail on Beaver Mountain just south of Rangeley," says Bill Ellis. "The trail was 3/4 of a mile long and had three big turns. We made about four runs in a day. It was only 1937 so we didn't even think about putting a lift in. We got a crowd of townspeople from Rangeley when we needed help cutting trails or when we installed a rope tow using a Model A engine on Gilman Hill in 1938," says Ellis. "Not many people skied, most of them viewed skiing as a nonsense sport. But some of us kids would start the tow and ski in the morning before school." The Rangeley lakes had long been a popular destination for summer tourists and the Rangeley Ski Club wanted to promote winter tourism. "Ski at 2,000' on season-round powder; uncrowded open slopes; 800' tow; day or night skating; sleigh rides; restaurants; hotels. Phone Rangeley 100," stated an ad in *Ski Illustrated* in 1947.

■ **RIVERSIDE WINTER SPORTS CENTER**—In the 1930s the municipal golf course on Riverside St. in Portland was used as a winter sports center. Ice skating and a double lane toboggan chute with floodlights were available. As a founding instructor of the Maine Professional Ski Association Avon Hilton gave demonstrations of ski techniques on the ski slopes.

■ **SUNRISE SKI SLOPE**—"I had never skied and wanted to learn," says Carleton Davis from Alexander, Maine. "It was the mid 1950s and I had a hard time finding skis to buy, then I found some with only a leather toe loop for a binding. I owned a campground on Breakneck Mountain and decided to build a rope tow. My area was the first one in the country to see the sunrise so I called it Sunrise Ski Slope. I only charged 25¢ for a ticket in the beginning and never made any money." A couple of light snow years and the new sport of snowmobiling combined to close the area in the 1974.

■ **WHITE BUNNY SKI AREA**—The White Bunny Ski Area opened in the late 1940s a couple of miles out of Fort Fairfield. Each fall club members took a tire off a tractor and replaced it with one in which the thick tread had been cut to create a groove. The tractor was backed into a shed at the top, the rope looped around the tire and the lift was ready to run. Equipped with lights for night skiing, the area was open in the evening during the week and all day and evening on weekends. When people started using snowmobiles they stopped at the lodge for something to eat or drink. The tow closed at 10:00 but the warming shack stayed open till about 2:00 for snowmobilers. A T-bar replaced the rope tow, but maintenance became a factor that led to the areas demise in the late 1960s.